Limerick in Old Photographs

Seán Spellissy

GILL & MACMILLAN

Dedicated to
Barbara Bingham, Martin Breen, Paddy Brennan, Pádraig de Bhaldraithe, Thomas
Keogh, Jean Mulholland and Larry Walsh who, between them, provided most of the
illustrations that made this book possible.

Gill & Macmillan Ltd
Hume Avenue
Park West
Dublin 12
with associated companies throughout the world
www.gillmacmillan.ie

© 2003 Seán Spellissy
0 7171 2940 3
Design and print origination by O'K Graphic Design, Dublin
Printed in Malaysia

The paper used in this book is made from the wood pulp of managed forests.
For every tree felled, at least one tree is planted, thereby renewing natural resources.

A catalogue record is available for this book from the British Library.

1 3 5 4 2

The author's previous publications include:
Clare County of Contrast (1987)
Limerick: The Rich Land (1989)
A Portrait of Ennis (1990)
Suicide: The Irish Experience (1996)
The Merchants of Ennis (1996)
The Ennis Compendium (1996)
The History of Limerick City (1998)
The History of Galway, City and County (1999)
Ennis in old picture postcards (2001, 2002)
Window on Aran (2003)

Contents

Acknowledgments

Jean Mulholland had virtually persuaded me to write a pictorial book on the city of Limerick when Fergal Tobin of Gill & Macmillan asked me to prepare *Limerick in Old Photographs*. I told some of my friends about the project and Barbara Bingham suggested that I use some of her father's photographs as he, the late Roy McCormack (1924–2001), had photographed many of the older buildings before they were demolished. In the meantime Jean Mulholland had approached Pádraig de Bhaldraithe and asked him to supply material from his archives, The Waldron Collection. Martin Breen allowed me to choose from his own collection which included many of the photographs that the late Stan Stewart had given to Gerry O'Connell. Gerry had presented these to Martin several years before his death.

Tom Keogh deserves special mention in this list of acknowledgments as he is undoubtedly one of the greatest private collectors of pictorial Irish memorabilia that I know. He is also unstintingly generous with his collection, photographic skills and time. He copied all of the photographs I used in this compilation, and even more that I had considered using. Any time I needed information on a particular photograph I telephoned or called on either Tom or Tony Browne, Limerick's walking encyclopaedias, a title that could be shared by Tom O'Donovan, Brian J. Hodkinson, Liam Irwin, Des Ryan and Larry Walsh. I would also like to thank Larry for providing me with photographs from Limerick Museum.

I would like to acknowledge the help I received from my partner, Detta, who ensured that I had time off in which to complete this and two earlier books on Clare and Ennis. Thank you Detta, I could never have managed without you. I must also acknowledge the help received from Teresa Behan, Peter Byrne, Gus Burke, James Birch, Philip Bingham, Dick Cronin, Mary Coughlan, Peter Cronin (Snr), Peter Cronin (Jnr), Colette Cotter, Maureen Comber, Michael Cowhey, Edward Crawford, Patricia Cusack, Gerry and Annette Dore, Kevin Donnelly, Seán Daly, Pat Dempsey, Niamh Downes, Anthony Edwards, Noreen Ellerker, Pauline Fenton, Noel Gore, Tony Grant, John and Millie Hassett, Cormac Hurley, Debbie Jacobs, Seán Kelly, Jim Kenny, Cliodhna McGill, Billy McGuire, Maura McGreevy, Ger Madden, Gerald O'Carroll, Deirdre O'Dea, Noreen O'Neill, Frances O'Gorman, Gerry O'Donovan, Padraic O'Farrell, Pat and Caroline O'Brien, David O'Mahony, Robin O'Donnell, Gerry O'Sullivan, Patricia Pomeroy, Sonia Schorman, Michael Tiernan, Gerard Williams and Hugh Weir.

Introduction

Archaeology proves that people lived on the banks of the Shannon River and the site of the present city of Limerick from Stone Age times. The Alexandrian astronomer, Ptolemy, showed a place he called Regia on the site of the later city of Limerick in the earliest known map of Ireland which dates from about AD 150. History and folklore and mythology confirm the presence of earlier settlements here where a legendary character, Immar, Yvours or Yvorus is said to have founded a city, in 155. Carthann the Fair, an Eoghanacht chieftain, and his son, Eochaidh Bailldearg, were baptised in Singland in 434, supposedly by St Patrick, a saint who is generally associated with Ulster, Sligo, Mayo and part of north-west Galway. Limerick derives its name from either a variant of the Norse term *Laemrich*, *Hlimrek* or *Allymrick*, meaning the rich loam, land or soil, or a Norse corruption of the older *Luimneach*, a name that was originally applied to a portion of the Shannon River. An ancient poem of 561 refers to the body of St Cuimin Fada of Clonfert being brought up the *Luimneach* by boat. The placename *Luimneach*, which occurs frequently throughout Ireland, generally signifies a bare or barren spot of land and is only anglicised as Limerick in one other area, within the parish of Kilcavan in Wexford.

The Vikings founded the original port and town from which the modern commercial city evolved. In 812 they plundered a small settlement on an island formed by the encircling waters of the Shannon. They returned as traders, settlers and mercenaries and one of their number, Tamar Mac Ailche (Thormor Helgason), a Viking sea-king, established the first permanent stronghold on the island in 922. The island became known as *Odensay* (Odin's island) and *Inis an Ghaill Duibh* (the island of the dark foreigner), rather than *Inis Sibhton*, *Inis Uibhtonn*, *Inis Sipont*, *Inis Ubhdain*, *Inis Ibhtonn* or *Inis Sibtond*, the names under which the island appears to have been known until the arrival of the

Vikings. By the late 1300s the placenames of *Inis Sibtond* and *Luimnech* or *Luimneach* were virtually synonymous, but long before then King John had laid claim to the island which is still called King's Island to this day. The Shannon River has a catchment area that comprises one-fifth of the entire island of Ireland and the Vikings of Limerick appreciated this geographical feature. Their longships pillaged ecclesiastical settlements along the banks of the Shannon and its tributaries, were carried over or around the waterfalls or other obstacles, and raided the length of the Shannon, from its mouth to Lough Ree. Rival Vikings from Dublin were defeated by Tamar Mac Ailche in 924 and six years later he formed an alliance with another fleet of Vikings under the command of Ivar and his three sons, Dubhcenn (Black Head), Cú Allaidh (Wild Hound) and Aralt (Harold). Despite ongoing conflict with the Vikings of Dublin and the Dalcassians of East Clare, the Vikings of Limerick established a series of settlements scattered throughout the later Counties of Clare, Limerick, Kerry and Tipperary. There was a Viking fleet in virtually every harbour and landing-place in Munster, and by the middle of the tenth century the Vikings had started to integrate with the native Irish. They gave their names an Irish form, organised themselves in the same way as the Irish tribes and formed an uneasy trading alliance with their former enemies.

Munster was once dominated by a loose federation of dynastic groups known as the *Eoghanacht* or *Eoghanachta*, descendants of Eoghan Mór (or Mogh-Naudhat), who divided Ireland into two halves during the late second century. Eoghan divided his half, the southern portion, between several groups who ruled the occupied areas by planting vassal tribes in the defeated kingdoms. The *Dal gCais* (seed of Cas) or Dalcassians claimed descent from a third-century king of north Munster, *Tuath Mumhan* or Thomond. They were a branch of the western Déisi, the Déis Tuaiscirt, and the Eoghnacht established them in east Clare from 744 onwards. In 934 they were first recorded as the Dalcassians. They emerged from comparative obscurity in 943 when their king, Cinnéididh Mac Lorcan, allied his forces with those of Ceallachán, the Eoghanacht king of Munster. The two kings forced the Vikings to pay tribute, but in 944 Ceallachán turned on his ally and killed two of his sons. Cinnéididh

died in 951 and Ceallachán in 954. Mahon, Cinnéididh's son, seized
Cashel and the Eoghanacht territories in 964, using a mythological claim
to the Eoghanacht possessions. Mahon defeated rival claimants at the
battle of Sulchóid and sacked Limerick in 967. The Vikings rebuilt the
city and Mahon formed an alliance with the Vikings of Waterford, the Eli
and the Déisi. By 972 he ruled north and east Munster but was killed by
an alliance of the Eoghanacht, Uí Fidgente and Vikings of Limerick in
976. He was succeeded by his brother, Brian Mac Cinnéididh (941–1014),
a man better known to history as Brian Bóru (Brian of the cattle tributes).
It was Brian who had captured Limerick, for his brother, nine years
earlier. He had returned in 968 and forced its inhabitants to part with
some of their treasures and allowed them to remain in the city on
payment of an annual tribute of 11,680 gallons of wine. In 977 he
attacked Scattery Island (another Viking base), avenged his brother's
death, defeated the enemy alliance, forged an alliance of his own with the
Vikings of Waterford, suppressed rebellion in Munster, waged war against
the king of Tara, Maelsechnaill, and eventually agreed to divide Ireland
in two halves with Maelsechnaill in 997. He put down revolts in Leinster
and in 1002 he forced Maelsechnaill to submit. Brian Bóru became high
king of Ireland but was killed at the Battle of Clontarf on 23 April 1014.

Brian was succeeded by two sons, Teige and Donough, and a grandson,
Turlough, the first of Brian's descendants to use the surname *Ó Briain* or
O'Brien, meaning descendant of Brian. All three laid claim to the high
kingship but lacked their progenitor's ability, unlike Murtagh Mór
O'Brien who established a new capital in Limerick in 1100 and gave his
former capital of Cashel to the Church in 1101. During his reign the
territory of Thomond comprised most of what later became County
Clare, all of Counties Limerick and Tipperary, a region co-extensive with
the diocesan territories of Emly, Killaloe and Limerick.

The Anglo-Norman invasion of Ireland spread westwards from
Leinster and in 1172 Domhnaill Mór O'Brien swore homage and
allegiance to Henry II (1154–1189) at Cashel. He was the last O'Brien
king to rule from Limerick. His third son, Donnchadh Cairbreach
O'Brien, succeeded him in 1201. He realised that he could not hold all of

Thomond and Limerick city against the Anglo-Norman invaders and decided to move his capital and residence to a safer location. He built what was probably the last royal *dún* in Europe in *Inis Cluain Rámh Fhada* (the island of the meadow of the long rowing) between 1208 and 1216, a place now known simply as Ennis. From there his descendants reigned as kings of Thomond until 1543.

Limerick became an Anglo-Norman fortress: King John built a great castle to keep an eye on Thomond; William de Burgo defended the city against the Irish; and Anglo-Norman settlers flocked here for safety. The former Viking fortress became the new Englishtown and Limerick lived up to its motto for centuries afterwards, *Urbs Antiqua Fuit Studiisque Asperrima Belli* (an ancient city well-studied in the arts of war). Irishtown had come into existence during the reign of King John as the native Irish were driven out of Englishtown to settle on the southern bank of *An Ghabhal Beag*, the little branch of the Shannon River now known as the Abbey river. This area became part of the walled city from 1320 onwards as the fortifications of Limerick were extended to include Irishtown. The city contained within these walls resisted sieges by the Cromwelllian army in 1651 and the Williamite army in 1690. It surrendered to the Williamite siege of 1691, the last Jacobite stronghold to hold out against William of Orange.

The city broke out from behind its medieval walls from the 1760s onwards and a new Georgian city was developed to the south and south-west, Newtownpery. Limerick has continued to expand; it underwent urban renewal in the 1980s and 90s and derelict sites have virtually disappeared. Limerick is officially the fourth largest city in the Republic of Ireland because the Limerick County Councillors refused to recognise the necessity of extending the city infrastructure into the suburbs of Castletroy, Raheen, Plassey, Dromore, Newcastle, Bawnmore, Rossbrien, Dooradoyle, Gouldavoher, Ballykeefe and Mungret.

Limerick in Old Photographs

Thomond Bridge still looks as it did about 1900. It replaced an earlier bridge constructed to link King John's Castle in Englishtown with Thomondgate on the Thomond side. The first bridge on this site may have dated from 1185 and is said to have been erected for £30 (€38). Other records mention that the bridge was built in 1201. This first structure, however, collapsed in 1292 drowning eighty workmen who were rebuilding it under the direction of William du Prene. The bridge was rebuilt and remained in use until it was replaced in 1840, 546 years later. (Limerick Museum)

James Pain (1779–1877) utilised every second pier of the centuries-old Thomond Bridge when he reconstructed and rebuilt the present one. His survey and drawings date back to 1814 and work actually commenced in 1838, although the foundation stone was laid two years earlier. A Gothic-style toll-house can be seen to the left of the bridge and a series of steps at the northern end lead into Franklin's Quay (now part of Verdant Place). The military barracks is visible behind the walls in this picture postcard of the early 1900s, before the Easter Rebellion. (Tom Keogh Collection)

This photograph may date from the mid-1930s or later, as you can see an electrical light-pole above the third arch, from the right, of Thomond Bridge. The roof-line and chimneypots of the Villiers' Alms-Houses, St Munchin's Church (Church of Ireland), the houses built into the old city wall in Verdant Place, the toll-house, the Castle Street houses, the old bishop's palace and part of King John's Castle form a backdrop, from left to right. The tower on the right, the oldest of the castle's towers, had its roof removed to accommodate artillery in the 1600s. (Tom Keogh Collection)

This photograph dates from about 1900 and shows a waterfront scene that probably remained unchanged from 1883, when St John's Cathedral was built, to the 1960s. The tower of St Mary's Cathedral can be seen on the skyline to the left, and on the right, a good distance away, is the spire of St John's Cathedral. A brewery, brewery mill and the City Gaol occupied the site on which City Hall now stands, behind the County Courthouse on Merchants' Quay, the last building on the right. A new city courthouse and the Corporation offices are now housed in City Hall. (Tom Keogh Collection)

This photograph of Nicholas Street or Maine Street was taken some time before 1894 as the five-storey building to the left was purchased by the dean and chapter of St Mary's Cathedral in that year. It stood next to the Exchange, was built by the Galwey family in the 1500s, had a Dutch-gable façade added in the late 1600s, and was demolished by 1895. Galwey's Castle or Ireton's House were the two names by which the house was usually described. Henry Ireton (1611–1651), Oliver Cromwell's son-in-law, died here of influenza or pneumonia on 26 November 1651. (Martin Breen Collection)

This photograph dates from the 1950s and shows Excel Cleaners and Dyers on the corner of Merchants' Quay and Bridge Street. Bridge Street was known as Quay Lane until the New Bridge of three irregular arches was built for £18,000 (€22,855) in 1762. This was replaced by Mathew Bridge which was constructed between 1844 and 1846. The entrance to the churchyard of St Mary's Cathedral lies further uphill, beyond the now-demolished business premises and other houses levelled to extend Merchants' Quay. In 1991 Jim Kemmy (1936–1997) opened a new pedestrian entrance to St Mary's from the quay. (Limerick Museum)

The Cathedral Close of St Mary the Virgin is more familiarly known as St Mary's Cathedral. Limerick became an episcopal city under the O'Brien kings who ruled from here and its first bishop, Gilbert, presided over the Synod of Rathbreasail in 1111 as Papal Legate. Gilbert resigned his episcopate in 1140 and his former diocese was mentioned in Cardinal John Papiro's list of 1152. The original cathedral may have been located elsewhere by 1111 but was relocated on the site of the O'Brien palace in 1168, 1172 or before 1192, on the instructions of the king, Domhnall Mór. (Tom Keogh Collection)

The interior of St Mary's Cathedral has changed considerably in recent times. In this photograph one can get an impression of how it looked between the 1880s and the 1980s. The choir stalls, or misericords, in the foreground were carved out of oak between 1480 and 1500. Twenty-three of these choir stalls still survive, designed to tip up vertically revealing a shallow ledge on which clerical posteriors could perch and give others the impression that clerics were standing upright rather than resting. This photograph was taken before work on the reredos and surrounds, completed by 1907, had commenced. (Tom Keogh Collection)

This photograph of the nave and part of the chancel of St Mary's Cathedral dates from the first decades of the 1900s. The Earl of Limerick's carved stall is on the left, next to the Bishop of Limerick's which has an elaborate crown on its top. This view from the chancel would, later on, be obstructed by the siting of a choir-screen designed by Conor O'Brien (1880–1952) of Foynes, author, architect, yachtsman, voyager and gun-runner. The screen was erected back to front in 1921, a mistake that was corrected in 1997, seventy-six years later. (Tom Keogh Collection)

Limerick's first cathedral may have been located on the site now occupied by St Munchin's Church (Church of Ireland). The original church may have been founded in 561, was destroyed by the Vikings, was renovated and rebuilt throughout the centuries and retained an episcopal throne into the early 1800s. The present church dates from 1827 and is shown here in a photograph of the 1950s. It was designed by James Pain, erected at a cost of £1,460 (€1,853) and replaced an earlier church featured in a map of 1590. The Island Theatre Company has leased the renovated church since 1989. (Limerick Museum)

The Thomond Provision Company was owned by Albert Valentine Waterstone and his wife, Emily Alice. In this photograph of 1910 Emily Alice Waterstone is standing in the doorway of her business premises. She enjoyed her role as a grocer and provisions merchant and wrote a poem on aspects of the grocery trade, on 4 November 1910. Many of her customers featured in her poetry: Mrs Legg, Mrs Mack, Mrs Hughes, Mrs Davis, Miss Scott, Miss Carroll, Mrs O'Donoghue, Mrs Nash, Mrs O'Brien, Mrs White, Mr Gibb, Mrs Greenwood, Mrs Lamb, Miss Hodgson and Old Higgins. (*Limerick Chronicle*)

In this photograph of the early 1950s we can see a terrace of houses on the left. They faced on to Merchants' Quay, overlooking the Potato Market, and were built on land reclaimed from the Long Dock, the Quay or Great Quay, which was built about 1500. It derived its later name from the merchants who once congregated here to conduct business and the name was retained by the early nineteenth-century developers who constructed the new Merchants' Quay on land reclaimed from the old harbour. The houses on the left have disappeared, their place taken by a car park. (The Waldron Collection)

The Castle Friary or Bourke's House is said to have been built by king Domhnall Mór O'Brien after he had given his palace to the Church. Although the surviving machicolation proves that it had defensive features, it was not a typical tower-house and appears to have been a late medieval house. John Bourke, a Catholic alderman, owned the house during the 1650s and it was used as a Franciscan friary from 1730 to 1780. Most of the house was demolished when Athlunkard Street was built in 1824 and only the northern wall remained. The photograph dates from the 1950s. (Martin Breen Collection)

This photograph of Fanning's Castle may be dated to the 1950s, but the building itself was most likely constructed as a tower-house of the late 1500s. In 1651 it was the home of Dominic Fanning, the seventeenth-century mayor who was hanged by the Cromwellians for defending Limerick city. He was one of twenty-four people who were excluded by name from the benefits of the treaty drawn up by Henry Ireton and Major-General Hugh O'Neill. Twenty-two were actually executed, including Sir Geoffrey Galwey, whose house was occupied by Henry Ireton, Cromwell's second in command. (Martin Breen Collection)

Although the trees in front of the Villiers' Alms-Houses have long since disappeared, the houses look almost as they did in 1826. They were designed by the Pain brothers and paid for by the will of Hannah Villiers which was established in the Court of King's Bench on 12 December 1815. The houses consist 'of a centre and two projecting wings, the former being surrounded by a cupola; it contains apartments for twelve poor widows, each of whom receives £24 Irish [€30.47] per annum'. Only the electrification of the early 1930s changed the early nineteenth-century façade. (Martin Breen Collection)

In this photograph of the Potato Market we can see the place as it looked shortly after it was restored by Limerick City Trust in the 1980s. The roofed, verandah-like structure in the background runs along the northern bank of the Abbey river and contained a small viewing balcony. This latter feature was removed a short time later when Sylvester O'Halloran (1728–1807) was commemorated with a footbridge across the river, which was opened in 1987. Sylvester was a surgeon who specialised in brain and eye surgery and developed a new method of treating cataracts. (Tom Keogh Collection)

This picture shows some of the older buildings on George's Quay as they looked when Stan Stewart photographed them in 1950. They were occupied at the time, as several children can be seen playing in the hallway on the right, while a woman looks down at them from an upstairs window. A mother and infant stand in the next doorway, beside a third doorway in which a man is lounging. The semicircular niches above the attic levels on three of the houses resemble, but are not, Dutch gables. All four were part of an early Georgian terrace of the 1760s. (Martin Breen Collection)

The women's section of the old City Gaol was photographed from the tower of St Mary's Cathedral in the early 1980s. The jail was built in Dean's Close in 1813 and was erected to replace another jail that had been established on the site of the Tholsel in 1750. Elizabeth Fry (1780–1845), a Quaker minister and prison reformer, remarked on how well regulated, clean and orderly Limerick Gaol was in the 1830s. Most of the jail was demolished in 1988, but part of the front façade was retained, including the 'drop-window' on Crosbie Row where prisoners were executed. (Barbara Bingham Collection)

This photograph of the 1980s shows a series of corporation houses and the Georgian barracks within the walls of King John's Castle. In 1935 Limerick Corporation erected twenty-two houses within the castle walls. These houses were demolished in 1989 and major archaeological excavations took place between that year and 1995. The Georgian barracks, the last of ten such structures built after 1751, was removed and the remains of a medieval building, the 'banquet-hall', but more likely the original keep, were found. Thomond Weir crosses the River Shannon, forming an attractive background, with Woodcock Hill to the left. (Barbara Bingham Collection)

Island View Terrace, looking down towards the junction with Island Road and St Ita's Street to the left. The low wall in the background, opposite the exit from Island View Terrace, has a gateway to the left which leads to a military cemetery that dates from 1856. The former gate-house that controlled access to the cemetery was the last house on Island Road until St Mary's Park, in St Mary's Parish, was built in 1935. Maureen Sparling, author and poetess, now resides there. This photograph seems to date from the 1960s, judging from the cars and people's clothing. (Michael Cowhey Collection)

This is a photograph of Limerick writer and historian Des Ryan. It was taken on the ground floor of the new Limerick Museum which is now known as the Jim Kemmy Municipal Museum, in honour of an outspoken activist, historian, politician and writer who was one of Des Ryan's closest friends. Des has written extensively on the Jews in Limerick, the pogrom or economic boycott that Fr John Creagh (1870–1947) waged against them, the suicide of Elsa Reininger (1882–1938), the Munster Fusiliers, the Blueshirts, the Spanish Civil War, and various aspects of military and republican history. (Tom Keogh Collection)

King John's Castle may have been erected as early as 1185, but security has been an on-going problem over the centuries. Note the difference in style between the sword-wielding Tom Keogh and his chain-mailed colleagues of another day, as they pose in the courtyard in 2002. The gate-house and its two flanking towers can be seen in the background. The unlikely looking structure to the right is a light-metal framework erected on the site of the former bartizan. This houses the reception area and interpretative centre and was built to protect the archaeological features discovered beneath. (Tom Keogh Collection)

This photograph was taken in Shannon Fields by Thomas Keogh Snr in 1950. His three young children can be identified, from left to right, as Thomas, Marie and Brendan. It was only recently that Thomas Jnr realised that the table tennis bats he and his brother are holding were probably made by their father. Shannon Fields are located between the Shannon River to the east, Lower Park Road to the west, Athlunkard Bridge to the north and the canal to the south. This was a popular recreational area in the not too distant past, into the mid-1970s. (Tom Keogh Collection)

This photograph dates from the 1980s when the Island Field was flooded by the waters of the River Shannon. The two youngsters on horseback appear to be having the time of their lives and other children can be seen in the background, either paddling or sitting on garden walls. The pony seems to be enjoying the spectacle as well! It looks relaxed as it wades through the floodwaters with its exuberant young riders. The Island Road could almost be classed as the frontier that separates the once-walled Englishtown from the rest of King's Island, including the Island Field. (Tom Keogh Collection)

This photograph was taken by Thomas Keogh Snr from the top tenement of No. 2 Creagh Lane during the late 1940s. His home overlooked part of the former City Courthouse which was erected between 1763 and 1765 at a cost of £700 (€889). Gerald Griffin (1803–1840) witnessed the trials of John Scanlon and Stephen Sullivan in this building. Both men were executed for the murder of Ellen Hanley (1803–1819), the Colleen Bawn. It became a Christian Brothers' school in 1846 and Thomas Keogh Snr captured Brother Matt White giving pupils a lesson in basketball almost a century later. (Tom Keogh Collection)

The Thomond Shoe Repair Service stood on the corner of Nicholas Street and St Peter's Street and was photographed by Roy McCormack before its demolition in the 1980s. Nicholas Street derived its name from the medieval parish church dedicated to St Nicholas of Myra, the saint popularly known as Santa Claus. The Stix Restaurant, formerly the Thomond Cinema, now stands on the site of the church. St Peter's Street takes its name from Peter's Cell, an Augustinian nunnery founded by Domhnall Mór O'Brien in 1171. Part of the ruined convent was converted into the Peter's Cell Theatre before 1760. (Barbara Bingham Collection)

St Mary's Convent was built on the site of St Saviour's Dominican Friary, the wall of which can be seen between the convent building and St Munchin's Church (Church of Ireland) in the background. Donnchadh Cairbreach O'Brien founded the friary in 1227. This photograph dates from about June 1996 and most of the foreground has now been assimilated into the new Ring Road. Three Franciscan nuns established a convent and girls' school here in 1812, which faced on to Island Road rather than Bishop Street. Mercy nuns replaced the Franciscan nuns in 1838. (Tom Keogh Collection)

This photograph of Barrington's Hospital dates from the 1980s. Joseph Barrington (1764–1846) became a freeman of Limerick in 1819 and founded a hospital and infirmary on George's Quay in 1829. He was supported in this project by his four sons, Matthew (1788–1861), Daniel (1792–1842), Croker (1797–1844) and Samuel who was born in 1806 and died without issue. Joseph Barrington was created a baronet on 30 September 1831. He and his sons spent £10,000 (€12,697) on the construction of the hospital which continued to serve the people of Limerick until it closed down in 1988. (Tom Keogh Collection)

Athlunkard Boat Club is located north of the western end of O'Dwyer Bridge, its entrance guarded by wrought-iron ornamental gates that were presented by Archibald Murray in 1901. The gates were manufactured by Bethell's foundry-works at Watergate, contain copperwork motifs in the Celtic Renaissance style of the era, and were part of a set that stood at the entrance to Todd's Bow in William Street. The Athlunkard Boat Club was founded in 1898 and the bridge was known as Park Bridge until 1931. The clubhouse, situated on the banks of the Abbey river, was photographed in the early 1980s. (Tom Keogh Collection)

In this photograph one can see Athlunkard Bridge as Stan Stewart saw it in the 1950s. It was designed by James and George Richard Pain and was built between 1826 and 1830 at a total cost of £16,000 (€20,315). The five large elliptical arches span the River Shannon and connect Corbally with Athlunkard, *Áth an Longphuirt* (the town of the encampment or fortress). The O'Briens had an ancient *longphort* on the Clare side of the river and the Vikings established a settlement close to the original ford which was in the vicinity of the Lax Weir, a short distance downriver. (Martin Breen Collection)

This photograph of the early 1980s shows St Thomas's Island which is actually in County Clare with Athlunkard Bridge in the background, to the south-east. The famous Lax Weir is visible to the right of the island and may have been used by prehistoric man about 4,000 years ago. The name is of Scandinavian origin, from *lax* meaning a salmon, and was probably applied during the Viking occupation of 1,100 years ago. The weir is approximately 1,500 ft in length, stretches from the old mill at Corbally to the church at Parteen and was closed in the mid-1930s. (Tom Keogh Collection)

This photograph was taken by Stan Stewart about 1950 and shows several of the older buildings in Broad Street, a street once famous for its Dutch-gabled structures. Note the steep roof on the building just off-centre to the right. This was a typical roof of the kind found on most of the Dutch-gabled houses. The houses had been converted into tenements when the original owners left Irishtown, usually for Newtownpery, as Limerick expanded outside its medieval walls. Shops were often inserted into the ground-floor areas and two to three families occupied the upper floors. (Martin Breen Collection)

In the 1950s Stan Stewart photographed these buildings in John Street. The Launch Bar is now the name over J. Whelan's premises at No. 24, but the adjoining building, No. 23, now Spiders Hair Centre, is on the site of the original Brazen Head Inn. The name commemorates a red-haired woman who was killed near by as the Jacobite army defended the city against King William's Brandenburg Regiment. The principal inn on John Street was renamed in honour of the unknown heroine. It was rebuilt by Simon Kent in 1794 and still retains its commemorative plaque in this picture. (Martin Breen Collection)

In this Stan Stewart photograph of the 1950s one can see four impressive seventeenth-century houses in the background. The photograph appears to have been taken from Curry Lane, part of which is in the foreground. The tall houses faced on to Broad Street, part of Irishtown. Broad Street probably derived its name from the actual width of the street. It was shown as a wide thoroughfare in a map of 1633, with the gable ends of several large houses, possibly some of those in the photograph, facing the main route through Irishtown. (Martin Breen Collection)

Roy McCormack photographed the Drapery Cash and Carry in Broad Street during the early 1990s. This is a street name that can be traced back to about 1750. The street extends southwards from Baal's Bridge before it finishes at the junction with John Street, Grattan Street and Mungret Street. In 1633 a map in *Pacata Hibernia* showed a terrace of nine two-storey buildings with their gables fronting on to Broad Street. The same map showed similar buildings elsewhere in Irishtown and in the adjoining Englishtown and can be accepted as proving that gable façades existed before the Dutch arrived. (Barbara Bingham Collection)

Stan Stewart took this photograph of the Citadel in 1958. The archway in front was part of the Outer Citadel, while the other archway gave access to the Inner Citadel. It was constructed as an extra fortification for Irishtown, a gate-building or sallyport from which John's Gate would be defended. The Citadel was built between 1590 and 1650, was damaged during the Cromwellian siege and was strengthened and repaired by Jacobite forces during the late 1680s. It remained in use as a military barracks until 1752 and has been incorporated into the fabric of two hospitals built since 1781. (Martin Breen Collection)

These Dutch gables behind St John's Square were photographed by Stan Stewart about 1958. Dutch settlers had been introduced into Clare by the Earl of Thomond who was busy colonising his native land with overseas tenants and tradesmen: James Vandeleur had settled in Sixmilebridge by the late 1630s; forty Dutch linen weavers settled in the city in 1661; Dutch merchants established businesses and homes within the port; John Clenett owned Clonmacken House in 1680; and the Verekers had settled in Cork and Limerick by the early 1600s. Dutch-gabled buildings reflected the building style favoured by immigrants from Holland. (Martin Breen Collection)

This photograph of St John's Cathedral dates from about 1900. The idea of building a cathedral for the Catholic population of the city originated in the early 1850s. An original suggestion to replace the high altar of the earlier St John's Church met with such enthusiastic support that proposals to build a cathedral went ahead. The foundation stone of the new Gothic Revival-type cathedral was laid on 1 May 1856 and the first Mass was celebrated during March 1859. The spire measures 308 ft 3 in. from the base to the top of the cross. (Tom Keogh Collection)

The interior of St John's Cathedral as it appears in this photograph of 1900 remained virtually unchanged until the early 1960s. It was consecrated by Cardinal Michael Logue (1839–1924), Archbishop of Armagh and Primate of All Ireland, on 21 June 1894. The cathedral was designed by Philip Charles Hardwick (1820–1890), but the high spire was the brainchild of two local men, Maurice and S. Hennessy. The cathedral replaced an earlier church that had been built in 1753 and had served as both a parish church and pro-cathedral. The cathedral faces on to Cathedral Place, formerly Nicholas Street. (Tom Keogh Collection)

This photograph was taken in the bottom yard of the Christian Brothers' School in Sexton Street, probably in 1987 to judge by the presence of young Mark Keogh, the only bareheaded musician in the entire band. Sexton Street derives its name from Edmund Sexton Pery (1719–1806), the man who spearheaded the development of Newtownpery. The naming of Sexton Street can be dated back to 1797, but it was also known as Pery Street in the past. On 2 June 1828 the Christian Brothers laid the foundation stone for their first Sexton Street school which opened on 28 May 1829. (Tom Keogh Collection)

In 1996 Tom Keogh photographed the Long Can and the Good Shepherd Convent from the tower of St John's Cathedral. Joseph Lancaster, a London-born Quaker, established a non-sectarian school here about 1806. This school was located behind what later became the church of the Good Shepherd Convent and gave the adjoining street a name which was corrupted from Lancastrian to Lancan to Long Can. The Christian Brothers bought the building for £200 (€254) in 1821, leased ground to the Good Shepherd Order in 1858 and eventually sold the rest of the site to the nuns in 1888. (Tom Keogh Collection)

This view of John's Gate was photographed from the tower of St John's Cathedral in 1996. The modern buildings in the foreground date from the early 1990s. The street on the left is John Street which meets New Road across from the north-eastern corner of St John's graveyard, near Stoney Thursday Corner where Mayor John FitzThomas Bourke was almost stoned to death in 1646. Just north of the piece of graveyard shown here is an old pub, now renovated, at Stoney Thursday Corner, a corner formed by John Street and another street leading into John's Square, Church Street. (Tom Keogh Collection)

This photograph was taken in the Markets Field, most likely in the early 1970s. In the background is an old infirmary that overlooked Mulgrave Street and was originally known as the New County Hospital. It was built for £7,100 (€9,015) in 1811 on what was then the New Cork Road. Between 1791 and 1832 the Government passed a bill allowing for the post-execution dissection of all criminals. Most of those hanged in Limerick, with the exception of John Scanlan in 1820, were brought here for dissection. The hospital closed in the 1950s after the Regional Hospital opened at Dooradoyle. (Tom Keogh Collection)

In 1996 Tom Keogh photographed the Markets Field from the tower of St John's Cathedral. Part of St Joseph's Psychiatric Hospital can be seen in the background to the right and Mount St Lawrence Cemetery is visible in the background to the left. Mulgrave Street runs into Blackboy Road, but only a fraction of the latter is shown in the photograph as it runs into the Pike, at the end of Greenhill Road, on the left. Jim Kemmy (1936–1997), author, historian, publisher, editor, stonemason, politician, socialist and humanist, was buried in Mount St Lawrence in September 1997. (Tom Keogh Collection)

In 1996 Tom Keogh took this photograph from the tower of St John's Cathedral. Part of St John's Hospital is visible in the foreground to the right. St Lelia Street, in the centre of the photograph, heads off northwards, is bisected by Old Clare Street almost midway, and then continues until it meets with Clare Street. St Lelia Street was originally named Nelson Street, to commemorate Admiral Horatio Nelson (1758–1805) who won the Battle of Trafalgar on 21 October 1805 and was killed in the process. Clare Street commemorates the Earl of Clare, John Fitzgibbon (1749–1802). (Tom Keogh Collection)

Flood Street, from the tower of St John's Cathedral, is one of several photographs that Tom Keogh took from this high vantage point in 1996. St Nessan's School is in the foreground to the left, at the junction of Flood Street and Downey Street, and some of the houses on Sarsfield Avenue line the bottom of the photograph. Flood Street derives its name from Joseph Mary Flood, a local historian and district justice, who became a freeman of Limerick in 1948. Downey Street commemorates Michael Downey who was killed at the Fair Green by the Black and Tans in May 1921. (Tom Keogh Collection)

Keane Street commemorates Lieutenant Thomas Keane, one of three IRA men captured in Ballysimon on Sunday, 1 May 1921. A lieutenant in C Company, Second Battalion, he was executed in Limerick on 4 June 1921, five weeks before the truce came into effect on 9 July 1921. The street is shown in the lower left quarter of this photograph taken by Tom Keogh in 1996 from the spire of St John's Cathedral. Part of Kilmurry Avenue is visible in the centre of the picture, as is the corner at which Keane Street meets with Downey Street. (Tom Keogh Collection)

The three monuments featured in this postcard of the early 1900s honoured, from left to right, Viscount Fitzgibbon, Patrick Sarsfield and Daniel O'Connell. Viscount Fitzgibbon was posted as missing, presumed dead, after the charge of the Light Brigade at Balaclava, on 25 October 1854. His statue was blown up by the IRA on 9 June 1930. Patrick Sarsfield defended Limerick city against the Williamite forces in 1690 and 1691 and his statue was placed in the grounds of St John's Cathedral in 1881. Daniel O'Connell's statue was erected in the Crescent in 1857 and cost £1,300 (€1,650). (Tom Keogh Collection)

In July 1958 Stan Stewart took this photograph from the roof of St John's Hospital. The hospital, nearby square, street, Catholic cathedral and Protestant church are named after an earlier church which occupied the site of St John's Church (Church of Ireland), which is prominently featured here. The original church has been dated to about 1200, featured in a drawing made by Thomas Dineley about 1680, and was last repaired in 1843. The present structure was designed by Joseph Welland, built in 1851 and 1852, and consecrated on 24 June 1852. It fell into disuse in the early 1970s. (Martin Breen Collection)

This photograph dates from the early 1960s as the two houses on the left, Nos 1 and 2 St John's Square, were still occupied. The buildings were later acquired by Limerick Corporation and housed the City Museum from 1977 onwards. The square derived its name from St John's Church and graveyard and was the city's first Georgian development. The idea may have originated with John Purdon of Tinerana, was encouraged by Edmund Sexton Pery who went into partnership with him, and the square, containing eight houses, was constructed between 1751 and 1757. (Barbara Bingham Collection)

The Lock Mills can be seen to the left of the canal in this picture of about 1900. The Shannon Navigation sign on the right is a reminder of the regular steamboat service introduced into the canal system in 1815. The Irish House of Commons had proposed that the Shannon be made navigable from Limerick to County Leitrim in 1697. Work commenced in 1755 and by 1786 eighty miles of river were navigable, between Killaloe and Roosky. The first boats began to ply between Killaloe and Limerick in 1799, but this trade had almost ceased by 1904. (Limerick Museum)

The Lock Mills were built by Andrew Welsh and Edward Uzold between 1762 and 1764 for a total of £6,000 (€7,618). In June 1757 workmen started to cut their way through Bartlett's Bog, the Limerick Navigation Company was set up in 1767, and the Lock Mills were in a convenient location to exploit the newly developed canal. By the 1950s most of the Lock Mills had been demolished, Coras Iompar Éireann stopped using the route via the Grand Canal, officially, on 31 December 1959, and the Guinness Company ran the last cargo barge out of Limerick on 18 May 1960. (Limerick Museum)

This postcard of Sarsfield Bridge dates from about 1900 and shows, on the right, a length of Howley's Quay, Harvey's Quay and the archway leading to Honan's Quay, free of motor traffic. The tide seems to be out at the time the photograph was taken. The jetty on the right was part of the lock that served the swivel-bridge and gave access to craft utilising the upper reaches of the river. It is known locally as the Poor Man's Kilkee as the earliest excursions to Kilkee left from here and those who could not afford the trip stayed behind. (The Waldron Collection)

This postcard depicting the Shannon Rowing Club, with Sarsfield Bridge on the right, dates from 1930. The club premises is located on a man-made island that served as a bulwark to the western side of the lock and is known as either Wellesley Pier or Shannon Island. The Limerick Boat Club has its premises on the southern end of the island, on the other side of the bridge. The former club was established by Sir Peter Tait in 1868, while the latter was founded in 1870. Charles and Croker Barrington introduced eights rowing into Limerick some time after 1870. (The Waldron Collection)

The Sarsfield Bridge Memorial commemorates the Easter Rebellion of 1916. This is located on the plinth of an earlier monument dedicated to John Charles Henry, Viscount Fitzgibbon, who was posted as missing, presumed dead, after the Charge of the Light Brigade on 25 October 1854. Attempts to vandalise the Fitzgibbon monument were thwarted, but it was eventually blown up by the IRA on 9 June 1930. The explosion left the plinth intact and this was used to commemorate the rebellion. Kathleen Daly (1879–1972) of Frederick Street married Thomas J. Clarke (1858–1916), a leader of the Easter Rebellion, in 1901. (Barbara Bingham Collection)

This postcard of Sarsfield Bridge and Sarsfield Street dates from about 1950. The bridge, street and Clontarf Place were originally named after Richard Wellesley (1760–1842), second Earl Wellesley, the older brother of Arthur Wellesley (1769–1852), first Duke of Wellington. Richard was appointed as Lord Lieutenant of Ireland in 1821, a position he still held when an Act for the building of the bridge was passed in 1823. The famous tobacco firm, the House of Garryowen, can be seen to the left. It was demolished to make way for Dunnes Stores and a new link road to Arthurs' Quay. (The Waldron Collection)

The Imperial Bakery was located at 24 Sarsfield Street when Roy McCormack took this photograph in the early 1980s. The premises featured in many of the early twentieth-century guides to Limerick city and now houses a branch of the Trustee Savings Bank. Sarsfield Street was originally known as Brunswick Street, in honour of the English royal family, descendants of George I (1660–1726). He was the son of Ernest Augustus, Elector of Hanover, and Sophia, Princess Palatine, the granddaughter of James I (1566–1625). George was Elector of Hanover and Duke of Brunswick-Luneburg when he became king. (Barbara Bingham Collection)

This 1950 photograph shows the front door of one of the houses in Arthurs' Quay. The cut-stone pediment, over a rectangular frame, is similar to another door in Bank Place as both of these Georgian terraces dated from the same period, the early 1770s. The railings on the left allowed a certain amount of light into the basement area, which was accessible only from the interior of the house. The basement vaults were constructed of brick or stone and were in two sections, one part beneath each house and a second part outside and underneath the street. (Martin Breen Collection)

The McGuire family firm was founded in Denmark Street during the early 1800s. The firm purchased the grain-stores, granary and mills of Reuben Harvey, acquired possession of the northern side of Francis Street, from the water up to and including part of Rutland Street, and opened a branch in the London Bridge area of London. The Francis Street Mill became known as the Indian Corn Mill as the McGuires were the first Irish millers to mill Indian corn or maize in this country. The McGuires bought another mill in Croom and opened the Croom Mills Bakery in Francis Street. (Limerick Museum)

Francis Street lies to the left in this photograph of Arthurs' Quay which was taken in the 1940s. The McGuire family owned the northern side of the street, a site now occupied by Sarsfield House, until they transferred their business to the Dock Road in 1970. Part of their holdings included the Black Oat Stores and the English branch of the firm was registered as Thomas McGuire and Co.. Grain was exported throughout the British Empire by the McGuires, whose family name is commemorated in the names of a wharf and street in the vicinity of London Bridge. (Martin Breen Collection)

This photograph of Arthurs' Quay was taken by Stan Stewart about 1950. The quay was built by members of the Arthur family who leased land from the Corporation soon after the Custom House was built in 1769. Patrick and Francis Arthur reclaimed land, constructed the new quay at their own expense, and erected a terrace of houses running the full length of their quay. They established two other terraces on what later became Francis Street and Patrick Street, streets in which they lived and are commemorated. The houses were four storeys high, constructed over basements built on marshy ground. (Martin Breen Collection)

In 1958 Stan Stewart photographed Arthurs' Quay, which had undergone many changes since the early Georgian terrace had been constructed. By 1920 several of the, at least, fourteen houses had been converted into shops on the ground floor and others, like those in the photograph, had new doorways added to give access to the apartments or tenements above ground level. It is also obvious from this photograph that the basements or cellars were still in use, despite the risk of damp or actual flooding. In *Angela's Ashes* (1996) Frank McCourt writes of a night he spent here in the 1930s. (Martin Breen Collection)

By the end of Queen Victoria's reign (1837–1901) Arthurs' Quay had declined in importance and many of the terraced houses had fallen into disrepair. Limerick Corporation filled in the harbour area in the 1970s. Michael Tiernan, a civil engineer, masterminded the construction of a major shopping centre on the triangular site visible in this photograph of 1988. John Sisk and Son constructed the Arthurs' Quay Centre between May 1988 and October 1989. A few of the terraced buildings on Patrick Street still remain and are visible here, close to where the main entrance was installed in late 1989. (Tiernan Properties)

Patrick Street, named after Patrick Arthur, as it looked in the 1950s. Many of the buildings on the left-hand side have been demolished and now form part of the Arthurs' Quay Shopping Centre. The Prescott dry cleaners, on the extreme left, no longer exists as a separate business premises. It was demolished to make way for the main entrance to the shopping centre from O'Connell Street. O'Connell Street, Patrick Street and Arthurs' Quay meet at the junction formed outside the entrance. The streetscape on the right-hand side has remained virtually unchanged since the early 1800s. (Tom Keogh Collection)

This photograph of Nos 2 and 3 Patrick Street dates from about 1900. These buildings, then occupied by Joseph Hartman and the City Furnishing Warehouse, are among the few terraced houses on the western side of Patrick Street to survive into modern times. Both premises appear to have been quite dark, despite gas lighting, as the man in the doorway of No. 3 is reading his newspaper in daylight. In those days the Paragon Boot Stores was at No. 1, Williams and Co. were at 4, E. Bowe in 5, J. H. Irwin in 6, and Quin and Co. occupied 7 and 8. (The Waldron Collection)

Patrick Street was photographed by Roy McCormack as the new shopping centre was under construction during the summer of 1988. Cannock's clock is visible to the left of centre, and Dunnes Stores supermarket, a sub post office and a chemist shop now occupy the ground-floor area, which is covered by the hoarding on the right. On the extreme left one can see part of a Georgian entreprenuerial development, some of the façade of Commercial Buildings on Rutland Street. This development at the junction of Patrick Street, Francis Street and Rutland Street dates to 1805 and cost £8,000 (€10,157). (Barbara Bingham Collection)

This garage in Arthurs' Quay dates from the 1970s and operated into the 1980s when the ground it occupied became part of a major development, the Arthurs' Quay Shopping Centre. In 1920 the Glentworth Garage Works in Lower Glentworth Street were the sole agents for Sunbeam and Rover cars. The firm stocked all the principal English and American cars and supplied commercial vehicles, agricultural tractors and lorries. The garage in Arthurs' Quay was located on the edge of a large car park, built on land that Limerick Corporation reclaimed by filling in part of the old harbour in the early 1970s. (Barbara Bingham Collection)

This photograph of Denis Clery's public house on Denmark Street can be dated to 1985. The young boy looking at the camera is Ross Keogh. Denmark Street, which has been known under its present name since at least 1770, had no association with the Danes of Limerick, or with Francis and Patrick Arthur who were timber merchants there in 1788. The street is most likely named after Prince George of Denmark who died in 1708. He was married to Queen Anne (1702–1714), the younger daughter of James II who succeeded to the throne after William III died. (Tom Keogh Collection)

The construction of the new shopping centre at Arthurs' Quay was photographed by Roy McCormack in late 1988. In this photograph part of the ground floor has been completed and work is well under way on the next phase, the first floor. To the left of the crane is the entrance to Ellen Street. There is a large gap at the corner of Ellen Street and Patrick Street where another old building had been demolished by then. It has since been replaced by another structure. Ellen Street derives its name from another member of the Arthur family. (Barbara Bingham Collection)

This photograph can be dated to 8 April 1919 as it shows the tricolour-covered coffin of Robert 'Bobby' Byrne being carried towards St John's Cathedral. The funeral procession has just turned from O'Connell Street into William Street, passing the Household Bazaar Company premises at the corner. Bobby Byrne was adjutant of the Second Limerick City Battalion, was imprisoned on an arms charge, instigated a riot in Limerick Prison to obtain political status for himself and his fellow-prisoners, and then went on hunger strike. Moved to Limerick Union Hospital, he was shot during an escape attempt on 6 April. (The Waldron Collection)

This photograph dates from 8 April 1919. It shows the funeral procession of Bobby Byrne proceeding through the streets of Limerick city. The coffin is just turning into William Street from O'Connell Street and is almost in the centre of the O'Connell Street thoroughfare which is bisected by Sarsfield Street and William Street. The large corner building in the background was then trading as J. McBirney & Co. at 134 and 135 O'Connell Street. It changed ownership and became known into modern times as Roches Stores. It has been extended, rebuilt and renovated since then. (The Waldron Collection)

The site of a collapsed building on the corner of William Street and O'Connell Street in the early 1980s. Nobody was injured. The ground-floor premises was a shoe shop run by the Saxone Shoe Company, while two deaf and dumb tailors had a clothing repair service on the first floor. Commercial travellers had their Clare Chamber on the floors above. The corner was known locally as Saxone's Corner before the house fell. It was rebuilt shortly afterwards and occupied by Benetton, a fashion store. Patrick Keane opened a jeweller's shop here, at 10 O'Connell Street, on 9 November 2002. (Barbara Bingham Collection)

This photograph of William Street dates from about 1910 or 1915. There is an early motor car in the bottom left-hand corner, behind the pony and trap. William Street derives its name from William Russell, a local merchant. In the early 1900s the Harris family had their principal business premises at 43 William Street and the rather aptly named William F. Pike owned the Yarmouth Fish Stores at 2 William Street. Horses and traps or carts were the predominant form of vehicular traffic in the street at that time, but the introduction of cheap motor vehicles soon changed this. (The Waldron Collection)

In this photograph of James Clune's tobacconist's shop can be seen the proprietor and his staff assembled before the camera, possibly about 1910. The shop was located at 59 William Street, while Clune's Tobacco Factory was situated at 22 Upper Denmark Street, which ran parallel with William Street. The tobacco firm was established in 1872, but both shop and factory closed in 1981. Four years later the Irish Permanent Building Society opened new offices on the site of the demolished shop. Much of Denmark Street consisted of warehouses built of coursed stone with small arched windows set in brick. (The Waldron Collection)

In this photograph one can see part of a religious procession walking along Patrick Street in the early 1900s. In 1940 Sean O'Faolain wrote: 'Limerick is always boasting that it has the biggest Men's Confraternity in the country. It is the only city outside Dublin, except Galway, where there is a Jesuit Community: but the SJs do not seem to add much to the culture of Limerick; why I do not know. There are also Redemptorists and Dominicans. Redemptorists are the great popular Hell-Fire-and-Damnation preachers . . . in the old tradition of the priest with the blackthorn.' (The Waldron Collection)

This view of William Street may be dated to some time before 1900 as the street appears to be cobbled. In the postcard it is referred to as Wilham Street and offers a rare view of Victorian Limerick. The first building on the right is the business premises of J. P. Newsom and Co. at No. 21. Some of the buildings adjoining it, in descending order, are Edward Browne's at No. 20, Guinane's Stores at 19, James Fitzpatrick's at No. 18, P. Herbert at 17, O'Sullivan's Medical Hall at 16, T. Power's at 15 and the Limerick Workmen's Industrial Association at 14. (The Waldron Collection)

Limerick Prison — at least this view of it — has not altered too much since Stan Stewart photographed it fifty years ago. It was designed by James Pain (1779–1877), an architect better known for his work on some of the big houses of Ireland. The polygonal tower in the centre had five rays of building, two of which are visible here diverging from it. The prison was constructed on three acres of ground purchased for £958 (€1,216) in 1816. Work on the site commenced in 1817 and the 'New County Jail' was completed in 1821 for £23,000 (€29,203). (Martin Breen Collection)

This photograph of William Street dating from the late 1920s shows how the motor car had impinged on the traffic scene. On the right hand-side is a sign, P. Gleeson and Son, on the gable at the entrance to Little William Street. On the opposite side of the street, beyond the shop awning, is the railed-off building that served as a barracks for the Royal Irish Constabulary. The Garda Síochána (guardians of the peace) were established as Civic Guards in 1922. They occupied Nos 4 and 5 William Street until they moved to Henry Street in 1977. (The Waldron Collection)

This photograph of William Street dates from the late 1940s or early 50s and was taken almost outside the Newsom premises at No. 20. Newsom's had long since acquired the Browne store which was adjacent to their original shop at No. 21. Carew's leather store is on the opposite side of the street at No. 55. There were two tanneries operating in the city at that time. William O'Donnell's was located off the Island Road, on King's Island, and Eugene O'Callaghan and Son had premises in John's Square and Lower Gerald Griffin Street. Both tanneries had closed by 1950. (The Waldron Collection)

This St Patrick's Day procession took place in 1903. Both city and county had, and still have, a great reverence for the national apostle. Folklore and legend associate him with seven distinct wells named in his honour at Ballinacurra, Cloncagh, Kilpeacon, Knockderk, Knocklong, Knockpatrick and the village of Patrickswell. There seem to have been two St Patricks, however, one a Roman missionary who arrived here in 432 and died in 461, and another of British origin who arrived in 465 and died about 490. Their missions were confined to Ulster and north Connacht, while the south was christianised by other saints. (The Waldron Collection)

This photograph dates from the early 1990s and shows all that remains of Cruise's Royal Hotel, an empty space on Nos 5, 6 and 7 O'Connell Street. The sign on the hoarding states that a new pedestrianised shopping street will open in October 1992 and will consist of 55 shops, 20 apartments and 340 car parking spaces. Cruise's Hotel, the Royal Mail Coach Hotel or the Bianconi Coach Station, was established in 1791. It catered for the stagecoach services of the era, adapted to the railway trade and catered for the motor clientele. The hoarding covers the entrance to Cruise's Street. (Barbara Bingham Collection)

Cannock's clock-tower featured in this photograph of 1922. It was a well-known meeting place into the 1950s and 60s as people often arranged to meet each other beneath 'the clock'. The original premises at 134 George's Street, now 139 O'Connell Street, underwent several changes of ownership since it was first built before 1800. Thomas Waller, the Scottish firm Cumine and Mitchell, John Arnott, George Cannock, Peter Tait, Michael J. Cleary and James Moriarty Tidmarsh each owned the property between 1840 and 1871. Cannock's acquired the adjoining premises, 137 George's Street, and erected the distinctive clock-tower in 1888. (Tom Keogh Collection)

Jim Kemmy (1936–1997) published an article on the late P. J. 'Cushy' Ryan (c.1904–1974) in the winter edition of *The Old Limerick Journal* in 1981. Cushy Ryan joined the Free State Army during the Civil War. He may even have served on this barricade shown outside Cruise's Royal Hotel in July 1922. 'He was strongly anti-Republican at this time', Jim Kemmy wrote, 'and regarded most of the people who opposed the Treaty of 1921 as misguided.' He joined the IRA in the late 1930s as he considered Éamon de Valera a 'cunning Machiavellian politician'. (The Waldron Collection)

Free State soldiers erected barricades in O'Connell Street in July 1922. This photograph shows a barricade outside Cruise's Royal Hotel, placed there shortly after three companies of Free State soldiers entered the city unopposed, under the direction of Captain Timmy Murphy and Captain Troy, both of Limerick city, and Captain Lynch of Caherconlish. Cushy Ryan (c.1904–1974) lived throughout the Republican and Free State occupation of his native city but died before he saw his manuscript, 'The Fourth Siege of Limerick', in print. It was published in *The Old Limerick Journal* in the winter edition of 2002. (The Waldron Collection)

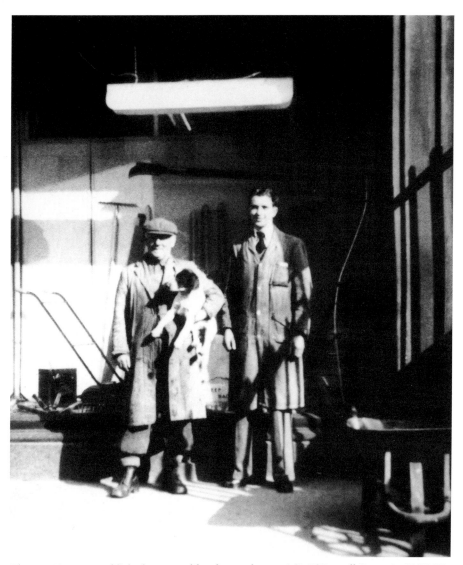

Thomas Hassett established a general hardware shop at 140 O'Connell Street in 1877. He sold his premises to Tyler's and moved to 9 O'Connell Street, where he was assisted by his sons, William (general hardware), Jim (plumbing and plumbing contracts) and Henry (radio). Desmond Hassett (1910–1988) and his brother-in-law, John Pomeroy (1929–1997), ran the business, had a fire on the premises in May 1956, and sold the property to Eason's in 1968. Roy McCormack took this photograph before the business was transferred to Ballinacurra. The 'literally nuts and bolts' hardware is now strictly trade. (Barbara Bingham Collection)

This postcard dates from about 1900 and shows O'Connell Street, which was then known as George's Street, a name it retained until 1917. The street was originally named in honour of George III, the English king who was determined to suppress revolution in the Americas and prevented Catholic emancipation between 1801 and 1807. Ironically, the street was renamed in honour of Daniel O'Connell (1775–1847), the emancipator of the Catholic population. George III is remembered in history as Mad George, whilst Daniel O'Connell is regarded as one of the greatest demagogues of his era. (The Waldron Collection)

The Ford cars in this postcard of O'Connell Street date it to the early 1920s. By then George III was but a distant memory and the revolution in Ireland had undermined the idea of an English empire. An Irish Free State had emerged in the aftermath of the War of Independence and the Civil War that followed, but it did not necessarily mean prosperity for all. Horses and carts or traps were still the most prevalent means of transport in those days, as evidenced in this picture. (The Waldron Collection)

In this photograph of the late 1940s from the steps of the Limerick Institution a group of people are looking at a parade passing through O'Connell Street. It may have been part of a St Patrick's Day parade as Eugene O'Callaghan and Sons have mounted an exhibition of leather hides on the back of a truck. The City Tannery, which was located in Lower Gerald Griffin Street, burned down in 1950 and never re-opened. The firm remained in business as wholesalers dealing in, but no longer tanning, leather hides, and operated out of a premises in John's Square. (Tom Keogh Collection)

This photograph dating from the early 1900s shows two of Henry Ford's cars on O'Connell Street. The impressive building on the left, on the corner of Glentworth Street and O'Connell Street, is one of several banks that were established in what is generally described as the commercial heart of the city. In the early 1900s there were five banks in O'Connell Street. These were the Provincial Bank of Ireland at No. 63, the National Bank at 94, the Bank of Ireland at 95, the Munster and Leinster at 107 and the Ulster Bank at 115. (The Waldron Collection)

The Kidd surname may be a derivative of an English nickname meaning a kid or young goat, or a variant of the diminutive Kit, a shortened version of Christopher or Katherine. In the early 1870s James Kidd of Dundee worked for James Fyfe, a licensed grocer at 4 George's Street, Limerick. He married his employer's daughter, took over the family business and opened two other branches, one at 103 George's Street and another at 18 Church Street, Ennis. His son, William, succeeded him and it is William's name that is on display above the assembled staff of No. 4, about 1910 or so. (The Waldron Collection)

John Patrick O'Mahony founded this shop at 120 O'Connell Street in 1902, the year in which this photograph was taken. The shop had a floor space of 450 sq. ft and sold books, stationery, ordnance survey maps, suitcases, shopping bags, postcards, souvenirs, pictures, religious pictures and statues, prayer books and missals. Picture framing was one of the supplementary lines that augmented income. Almost a century later Frank McCourt would state 'The best way to return to Limerick is to write a best-selling memoir, *Angela's Ashes*, and have its Irish launch in O'Mahony's Book Shop.' (David O'Mahony)

In this photograph of 1952 one can see how O'Mahony's façade has changed over a fifty-year period. It has altered radically since then. In 1996 the entire building was extensively renovated and emerged with over 10,000 sq. ft of retail selling area. A neighbouring pharmaceutical firm, Power and Mangan's, sold a yard to the O'Mahonys, which added another 5,000 sq. ft to the bookshop, turning it into the largest independent bookselling operation in Ireland. The O'Mahony family still controls the business and has branches in Limerick University, Ennis and Tralee, and a separate operation in Cork. (David O'Mahony)

This view of O'Connell Street seems to date from about 1940, to judge by the various cars shown here. It was photographed from the corner of Cecil Street, probably from the site of Bill Hanley's chemist shop. Two blinds, on the left, extend from another chemist's premises. The two figures above the blinds are of angels that have long since been moved to Bray. The large building next door is the Royal George Hotel, named after a paddle-steamer that operated between Cappa and Limerick. Another blind beyond the hotel extends from the Leverett and Fry grocery store. (The Waldron Collection)

This photograph may date from about 1910, or even earlier, and was one of a collection that Stan Stewart gave to Gerry O'Connell. The former carriage-building firm of Christy advertised as a motor works in the trade directories of 1913. It was located at 58 O'Connell Street, a few doors away from the *Limerick Leader* offices. Christy's is now the site occupied by the Limerick County Library, but a few of the city's older citizens remember petrol pumps on the pavement. A 'horseless carriage' was the term used to describe these first motor vehicles. (Martin Breen Collection)

This view of O'Connell Street dates from the early 1950s and shows the Woolworth and Co. department store on the right-hand side. The Royal George Hotel is to the left, next to the Leverett and Fry grocery store, which stood on the corner of Roches' Street. Michael Wogan, Terry Wogan's father, managed the Leverett and Fry establishment. Terry was born at 18 Elm Park, north of the Ennis Road, on 3 August 1938. Richard St John Harris, another famous Limerick celebrity, was reared in 'Overdale', on the Ennis Road, the city's most exclusive residential area. (Limerick Museum)

Stan Stewart took this photograph of the Adare coach in 1941, as it wound its way up O'Connell Street towards O'Connell Crescent. The young boy on the bicycle seems to have been the only one present who was aware of the photographer. The coachman, in top hat, seems to be delivering a lecture to his attendant passengers or simply standing up to put on an overcoat. In comparison with our times these horses are in very poor condition. They look badly nourished and have protruding hip-bones. (Martin Breen Collection)

This postcard of St Joseph's Church was produced shortly after the building was opened on 24 April 1904. The church was designed by William Corbett, the city surveyor, who oversaw the construction of the Redemptorist Church and residence in 1858. He designed the Tait Clock in 1867 and the Franciscan Church in 1876. St Joseph's Church is located on Limerick's shortest street, Quinlan Street, which is between O'Connell Crescent and O'Connell Avenue. It derived its name from Thomas Quinlan who constructed two houses, Nos 1 and 2, here. South's pub, mentioned in *Angela's Ashes* (1996), is No. 4. (The Waldron Collection)

O'Connell Avenue is now the name of Military Road, shown in this postcard of the early 1900s. When the New Barracks, now Sarsfield Barracks, was built on South Prior's Land in 1798, it was located to the south of the Georgian town. This meant that the soldiers had to march to church or form military parades as they passed to or from the city. Such parades were used to provide a certain amount of entertainment, impress visitors and locals alike with military strength and, of course, to recruit young men into service within the ranks of an imperial army. (The Waldron Collection)

This doorway on Bank Place, and the building into which it led, was in a ruinous condition by the early 1980s. Bank Place derived its name from the Bank of Limerick or Maunsells' Bank which was established at No. 6 in 1789 by Thomas Maunsell (1732–1814) of Plassey, his brother, Robert Maunsell (1745–1832), and his brother-in-law, Sir Mathew Blakiston (1760–1806). Robert Maunsell was brought up in India, held a writership in the Madras Presidency, was fourth in the Council at Ganjam, and returned to Limerick after his wife, Anne Maxwell Stone, inherited a fortune in 1789. (Tom Keogh Collection)

The Sarsfield Bar, at 1 Rutland Street, stands at the corner of that street and Bank Place. The Georgian street commemorates Charles Manners (1754–1787), fourth Duke of Rutland and Lord Lieutenant of Ireland, who visited Limerick in 1785. Peter O'Brien (1799–1855), uncle to Peter 'The Packer' O'Brien, once had his wine stores here in this building, now the property of Seán Hickey. The building next door, No. 2, had disappeared by 1990 when this photograph was taken. Pat and Caroline O'Brien opened the Celtic Bookshop beside the Sarsfield Bar in 1995. (Tom Keogh Collection)

This ruined doorway was once the entrance to Bruce's Bank in Rutland Street and is a more elaborate form of the doorways associated with St John's Square. This photograph dates from the early 1980s, not long before urban renewal transformed or obliterated parts of the city. George Evans Bruce opened his own bank, George Evans Bruce and Co., in 1806, in partnership with Eyre Evans and George Bruce Evans. In 1816 he was satirised in a poem, 'The Nosegay', by Thomas 'Spectacles' O'Grady. The bank closed in 1820, but all of the creditors were paid in full. (Tom Keogh Collection)

Roy McCormack photographed Ellen Street in the 1970s. In 1805 the street derived its name from Ellen Arthur, one of the family that built Arthurs' Quay, Francis Street and Patrick Street. The Arthurs were of Viking or Norse origin, occasionally used the Norman prefix 'Fitz' and were settled in Limerick long before the Anglo-Normans arrived. Members of the family prospered as merchants and the Arthurs held mayoral office fifty-eight times between 1218 and 1635. During the Cromwellian period some of the Arthurs were deemed ineligible to be citizens of a walled city because of their Catholicism, and moved to Ennis. (Barbara Bingham Collection)

This photograph of the US Bargain Stores in Parnell Street can be dated to the 1960s. Standing in the doorway, from left to right, are John Conway, his wife, Marie, and sister, Sarah. Tom Keogh worked there as a youth and witnessed many of the changes that have taken place in the city since then. Parnell Street was originally named Nelson Street after Horatio Nelson (1758–1805) who was created Baron Nelson of the Nile in 1798 and Viscount Nelson in 1803. It was renamed in honour of Charles Stewart Parnell (1846–1891) who was made a freeman of Limerick in 1880. (Tom Keogh Collection)

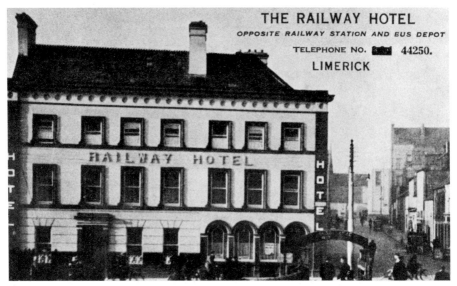

This postcard advertising the Railway Hotel can be dated to the late 1930s or early 40s. The building is located at the corner of Boherbuoy and Davis Street. Boherbuoy is a derivative of *Bother-buidhe* (the yellow road). Davis Street was originally named Queen Street, after Queen Victoria, but renamed in honour of Thomas Osbourne Davis (1818–1845), poet, patriot, journalist and Young Irelander. (Limerick Museum)

In 1804 Nelson Street was named in honour of Horatio Nelson (1758–1805) who was created a viscount in 1803. The original address of 18 Nelson Street had changed to 18 Parnell Street when this photograph was taken in 1935. The two men standing outside the shoe repair shop of M. Wallace are wearing heavy, possibly leather, aprons. This would indicate that they were working in, or possibly owners of, the premises. W. Wallace and Sons were listed in a directory as 'shoe retailers and repairers' at 2 Lower Henry Street nearly thirty years later. (Tom Keogh Collection)

The Leamy Free Schools were established by William Leamy, an adventurous Limerick seaman, most likely a pirate, who left £13,300 (€16,887) for the education of the poor of his native city. He made his will in 1814, died on Madeira and this school opened in Hartstonge Street in 1844. William Leamy stipulated that it should be multi-denominational, but Rev. Edward Thomas O'Dwyer (1842–1917), the Catholic Bishop of Limerick from 1886 onwards, turned it into a Catholic school in 1894. Frank McCourt was educated here, but the school closed and was a clothing factory by the 1950s. (Martin Breen Collection)

John Kenny had established his business at 14 Upper Cecil Street by the early 1900s. This photograph was taken about 1950. It shows what was then a new well-maintained building owned by John Kenny and Son, Builders. Signs on the front advertise that there is a joinery works within, one in which school and church furniture, doors, windows, frames and sashes can be made to order. Cecil Street derived its name from Rev. William Cecil Pery (1721–1794) who was consecrated Bishop of Killaloe in 1781, became Bishop of Limerick in 1784 and was created Baron Glentworth of Mallow on 21 May 1790. (Limerick Museum)

The Matterson surname is one of those Limerick names that is synonymous with the bacon industry within the city. This photograph of the J. Matterson buildings dates back to about 1950. Every part of the pig (except its squeal!) was used by the four main bacon factories, Denny's, Matterson's, O'Mara's and Shaw's. Pig meat of every description was sold in neighbouring shops. Some of the bladders were blown up and given to the children to use as footballs. Limerick workers went to Russia to teach the Russians how to slaughter, preserve, smoke, pickle and slice bacon. (The Mulholland Collection)

This photograph of Matterson's staff dates from the early 1900s, a time when the bacon industry was at its peak in Limerick. Pigs were brought into the city from almost every county in Ireland and exported throughout the British Empire as prepared bacon, ham and pork products. In 1975 Jim Kemmy (1936–1997) wrote an article in the *Limerick Socialist*, in which he regretted the lack of documentation on the pig-buying families, such as the Crowes, O'Connors, O'Donovans, Reids and Sheahans, and mentioned how many people in the working-class areas of the city kept pigs in their backyards. (Limerick Civic Trust)

The Limerick Savings Bank is known locally as the 'Stone Jug' and has altered little since Stan Stewart photographed it in 1950. The railings around it have disappeared, but the building still serves its original purpose. W. H. Owen designed the Doric temple-style structure, with four fluted columns, soon after the Earl of Limerick leased land in Upper Glentworth Street to the Limerick Savings Bank in 1839. The bank was founded in 1820 to provide the ordinary people of the city with a chance to save money. The Trustee Savings Bank continues this tradition with Seán Crowley as manager. (Martin Breen Collection)

The staff of Denny's bacon factory posed for this photograph in the early 1900s. The families that operated the four main factories were the merchant princes of their era, but other people associated with the trade prospered at the same time. Farmers and pig-buyers throughout Ireland shared in the prosperity at a national, provincial and county level. Within the city, local pig-buyers bought urban-bred or backyard pigs from friends and neighbours, particularly in the Athlunkard Street area. Pigs reared by tenants, country or city dwellers alike, were known as 'the gentlemen who paid the rent'. (Limerick Civic Trust)

This postcard photograph of the Glentworth Hotel may date from the 1890s. Note the hackney cab, one of the original horse and carriage type, at what is still the somewhat changed main entrance. The façade on the right faces on to Upper Glentworth Street, named after Baron Glentworth, while that on the left looks on to Catherine Street which takes its name from Catherine Unthank, a member of one of the mayoral families of Limerick. James Pain (1779–1877), one of the two famous Pain brothers, made his home here, while his brother moved to Cork. In 1846 James Pain was recorded as an officer of the North Munster Provincial Grand Lodge. (The Waldron Collection)

This postcard of 1898 or so shows St Saviour's Dominican Church which was designed by the Pain brothers about 1815. In 1863 a new chancel was constructed and the building was subsequently altered in 1870, 1898 and 1982. The Tait Clock, on the edge of Baker Place, is visible to the right, St Saviour's Church is on the corner of Glentworth Street and Dominic Street, and the two buildings on the left are on Pery Street. The first is Trinity Church, which now houses the Mid-Western Health Board, and the second is Hevergal Hall, the later Lyric Cinema. (Tom Keogh Collection)

St Michael's Church (Church of Ireland) was built to replace St George's Church on what was then (King) George's Street. It was designed to fit this location at the People's Park end of Barrington Street, with its eastern façade looking on to Pery Square. The church was consecrated in 1844, renovated in the 1870s, and appears to have changed little since it was photographed in the early 1900s. The street derives its name from the Barrington family, two of whom were investors in the Tontine Company that built Pery Square. The Samaritans moved from Cecil Street to Barrington Street in 1993. (The Waldron Collection)

Richard Russell, the owner of the Plassey Mill and Crescent House and a partner in the milling and grain firm of John Norris Russel and Sons, died in 1871. The People's Park was dedicated to his memory and opened to the public in August 1877. The park kiosk, on the Boherbuoy side of the park, was photographed by Cliodhna McGill in 1988, shortly before it closed down for good. All the enamel advertisements remained intact, advertising the former newsagency and tobacconist's which had served the local population for generations, until they were stolen in the early 1990s. (Cliodhna McGill)

This postcard of 34 Cecil Street dates from the early 1980s and shows the late Tom Collins standing in the doorway of his public house. His name appears on the fascia board above the premises. He shared his name with a cocktail, the Tom Collins, a drink popularised in the 1940s and 50s. Tom died soon after this photograph was taken and his widow died in February 2003. One of their sons, Michael Collins, is the artist responsible for executing the official mayoral portrait of the late Jim Kemmy (1936–1997), founder of *The Old Limerick Journal*. (Tom Keogh Collection)

This postcard dates from about 1900 in which one of the Waldron family noted that a group of people were assembling near the monument in the People's Park, possibly for a photograph. The monument in the centre supports a statue of Thomas Spring-Rice (1790–1866) who was Chancellor of the Exchequer from 1835 to 1839 and was created Baron Monteagle of Brandon in 1840. He coined the term 'West Briton', an expression that would assume derogatory overtones in the 1900s. 'He designated himself as a West Briton', wrote Richard Lalor Sheil (1791–1851) who added, 'He is more than English.' (The Waldron Collection)

This photograph of the archway leading into the Limerick Clothing Factory dates from 2000. The factory was established by a Scotsman, Peter Tait (1828–1890), and was located at 28 and 29 Lord Edward Street. This young entrepreneur from the Shetland Islands pioneered the use of steam and power-driven machinery to become a mass producer of ready-made clothing. During the American Civil War he produced uniforms for the Confederate Army in Limerick and sub-contracted orders for the Northern Army uniforms which he supplied from Leeds. He also supplied the entire British Army with uniforms. (Tom Keogh Collection)

In this photograph one can see the backs of 104 and 105 Henry Street, as they looked about 1950. The lorry shown here is travelling along Bishop's Quay which derives its name from No. 104, the residence of Bishop William Cecil Pery (1721–1794) in 1784. Both houses date from the 1780s and Michael Stapleton, a famous Georgian plasterer, worked on both. The Earl of Limerick, Edmund Sexton Pery (1719–1806), lived at No. 105 which is now known as Hibernian House. No. 104 became St Munchin's College and is now the office of the Greyhound Racing Board. (Martin Breen Collection)

This postcard of Laurel Hill Convent dates from about 1950. It was the only convent in the diocese of Limerick over which Edward Thomas O'Dwyer (1842–1917), the Bishop of Limerick, had no jurisdiction as it was a French foundation. It was established by Mother D'Hover, superioress of the Faithful Companions of Jesus, in 1844. These nuns were members of an order founded by Marie Madeline Victorie Bengy, the widow of Antoine Joseph de Bonnault d'Houet who died ten months after their marriage. Madame d'Houet spent six months in Limerick supervising the construction of Laurel Hill House and Convent. (The Waldron Collection)

The Redemptorist Church on South Circular Road, formerly part of Courtbrack, faces on to Quin Street, in this photograph of pre-electricity days, possibly the 1920s. The church and residence were built by a local builder, named Wallace, and supervised by William Corbett, the city surveyor. The high altar was designed by George Goldie of London and unveiled on 15 October 1865. The chief building material, magnesium limestone, was imported from France and Clare, and Sicilian marble was used in the interior. Quin Street, formerly Alphonsus Avenue, derived its name from the O'Gorman Quin family who sponsored the Redemptorists. (The Waldron Collection)

This postcard of the Church of St Alphonsus Liguori, better known today as the Redemptorist Church, dates from about 1950. The missionary Fathers of St Alphonsus, the Redemptorist Fathers, came to Limerick in 1851 to preach at a mission in St John's Church. They were invited back in 1852 and Dr John Ryan (1784–1857) gave them a foundation in 1853. They acquired a large field in Courtbrack, *An Cúirt Bhreac* (the speckled mansion or court), most likely Dewlishe or Delishe Castle or Ballinacurra Castle, in 1854. They erected a temporary chapel here and started to construct a residence in 1856. (The Waldron Collection)

Villiers' School was still in use for educational purposes when Stan Stewart photographed it, about 1958. The school was one of two founded and endowed by Mrs Hannah Villiers in her will of 1815. The school shown here was constructed in Henry Street, while another was built in Nicholas Street during the 1830s at a total cost of £7,500 (€9,523). By the 1860s the Henry Street school had a total of 94 pupils, 50 boys and 44 girls. There were fewer students in the Nicholas Street school which was conducted under the jurisdiction of the National Board of Education. (Martin Breen Collection)

Kyle House now occupies this site on Henry Street. The photograph, dating from 1982, demonstrates what the place looked like over twenty years ago. Urban renewal throughout the 1980s and 90s changed the face of Limerick in many respects, mainly for the better, thanks to men like Jim Kemmy (1936–1997) and Kevin Hannan (1920–1996), unofficial guardians of the city they loved. Henry Street derived its name from Edmund Henry Pery (1778–1844) who was created Viscount Limerick in 1800 and Earl of Limerick in 1803 and lived in 105 Henry Street. (Tom Keogh Collection)

This photograph taken at the corner of Clontarf Place and Upper Henry Street dates from 1982. One can see the entrance to a narrow cul-de-sac before the first car on the left. The buildings visible at the end of Clontarf Place are on the opposite side of O'Connell Avenue. Clontarf Place was originally named Wellesley Place, after Richard Wellesley (1760–1842), a brother of the more famous general who defeated Napoleon Bonaparte at Waterloo in 1815. Clontarf Place commemorates the Battle of Clontarf in which Brian Bóru (941–1014) defeated his Leinster and Viking foes. (Tom Keogh Collection)

Angela's is on the corner of Henry Street and Mount Kennett Place in this photograph of 1982. The original Mount Kennett was located to the west, an area between Windmill Street and Frederick Street (later O'Curry Street). Mount Kennett became famous for the lace that was produced here from 1829 onwards, when upwards of 300 women and children were employed by Charles Walker in his factory. Charles Walker teamed up with Samuel Lambert in 1840 but died in 1843. The firm he established prospered under the name of Lambert and Bury and employed 900 workers in the early 1850s. (Tom Keogh Collection)

John Russell (1766–1839), sixth Duke of Bedford, was Viceroy of Ireland in 1806. Bedford Row commemorates his appointment but has seen a lot of changes since then, as this photograph of the late 1970s shows. Calvin's Boys & Menswear advertises a drapery in the former Grand Central Cinema which was erected in a Gothic style in 1821. It was built as a preaching house for and by the Primitive Wesleyan Methodists of the city. The Independent Meeting House was constructed around the same time but is operating as another cinema, showing *Yanks*, a film starring Vanessa Redgrave, in this photograph. (Tom Keogh Collection)

This view of High Street was photographed by Tom Keogh while standing outside the Hackett Barber Shop, No. 20, in January 1988. Upper Denmark Street is to the left and the Round House can be seen to the right. The second building on the left is Seán McMahon's High Street Bookshop which is now re-opened on almost the same site. John O'Brien's bookshop and photographic gallery opened in 1989 and moved to 26 High Street in 2002. The Yellow Lemon Balti House now occupies the site of the first house and yard at the corner with Upper Denmark Street. (Tom Keogh Collection)

The New Barracks was erected on South Prior's Land in 1798. It was renamed Sarsfield Barracks and is surrounded by O'Connell Avenue, Roden Street, Barrack Hill, Wolfe Tone Street, Spellacy Square, Lord Edward Street, Prospect Hill, Fitzgerald Place and Verona Esplanade. At the time of the Civil War the barracks, barrack square, outbuildings and playing field covered an area of about ten acres. Two months after the British Army departed, it was occupied by Republican forces. They set it alight on the night of Thursday, 20 July 1922, and one can see the ruined garrison church in this postcard. (The Waldron Collection)

The Milk Market, from the Mungret Street side, has changed only slightly since this photograph was taken in the 1950s, but the surrounding area has altered beyond recognition. The former market buildings now house Sean Kelly's bookshop, a number of other business premises and a large car park. The Milk Market was originally designed and built as a corn market and gave its name to the row of buildings opposite the former main gate, Cornmarket Row. Carr Street, on the eastern side of the Milk Market, takes its name from the Carrs, a mayoral family of 1771. (Martin Breen Collection)

In the 1830s the flour mills of the city ground over 50,000 barrels of flour a year. John Norris Russell built a corn and maize mill in 1810. He fitted it with steam-powered engines in 1827 and added a nine-storey cornstore ten years later. He was one of several entrepreneurs who established Limerick as the centre of the largest flour-milling industry in the south of Ireland. In 1913 the city contained five large mills. Roy McCormack took this photograph in the late 1980s. The only mill operating in 1989 was O'Neill's of Upper William Street. (Barbara Bingham Collection)

Roy McCormack photographed the demolition of Rank's flour mills and cornstores in 1990. Rank's had purchased the interests of the Russell family in 1930 and later concentrated all their enterprises within one large complex on the Dock Road. The building on the right was completely demolished. The silo on the left, separated from the mills on the right by the Dock Road, once belonged to James Bannatyne. The silo is located in the dockyard near one of the few surviving six-storey grain stores, the Bannatyne building, which was designed by William Sydney Cox to hold 2,400 tons of cereal. (Barbara Bingham Collection)

Tom Keogh photographed the site of Rank's mills and outlying buildings in the early 1990s, a time when a new industrial estate was in the course of construction. Two of the Victorian mill buildings are visible in the background. The one on the right is a silo, while that on the left is a six-storey cornstore, the Bannatyne Building, which was constructed on a 6 ft-deep concrete foundation in 1873. The foundation was actually laid on a solid rock stratum that was 13–25 ft below the surface of the ground, close to the Limerick Docks. (Tom Keogh Collection)

This photograph can be dated back to about 1987 when the new Shannon Bridge was in the process of construction. Steamboat Quay has changed beyond recognition and the landmark premises of Denis Coakley had closed a number of years previously. Roy McCormack took this photograph. Taoiseach Charles J. Haughey officially opened the bridge on 30 May 1988, but it had already earned a new name for itself before that date. As gale force winds swept along the Shannon River on Tuesday, 9 February 1988, the new bridge emitted a whistling sound and became the 'Whistling Bridge' or 'Whining Bridge'. (Barbara Bingham Collection)

This photograph of a busy Limerick Harbour probably dates from the 1940s or even earlier. It was one of the photographs Stan Stewart presented to Gerry O'Connell in the 1960s. Some of the vessels shown still carried sails, but this may have had more to do with the economy practised during 'the Emergency' (World War II), when fuels were in short supply. The docker featured here is wearing a sack on his shoulder and another around his waist to protect his clothing. A Dockers' Mass is celebrated on the last week of each November in Dolan's nearby pub. (Martin Breen Collection)

This photograph of Troy's Lock and the canal was taken by Tom Keogh during the 1980s. The lock was located a short distance upstream from Park Bridge. The Troy surname is commemorated in the name of both this lock and a port, harbour or ferry, known as *Caladh Uí Throighthigh* (the *caladh* of the Troys). The *O'Troighthigh* (descendants of the foot-soldier), originated in, or close to, Corcomroe in County Clare. They spread into Offaly, Tipperary, Limerick and Cork and have been confused with the Anglo-Norman Troys of Waterford and Kilkenny. Castletroy is a corruption of *Caladh Uí Throighthigh*. (Tom Keogh Collection)

Tom Keogh photographed this cottage on the Canal Path, near Park Bridge, in the 1980s. This house was probably erected soon after work commenced on the canal in 1757 but is typical of others built outside the city walls, in a district known as Park. The area comprises the three townlands of Lower Park, Rhebogue and Singland, and was occupied by an ethnic group called the Park Danes, descendants of the Catholic Ostmen or Vikings driven out of the city by the Cromwellians. Costello, Cotter, Doyle, Godfrey, Hally, Harold, Hastings, Howard, Kenrick, MacAuliffe and Setright are amongs their surnames. (Tom Keogh Collection)

David Fitzgerald of Ballysimon is shown taking a jump at the Limerick Horse Show of the 1940s. Jack Ryan developed the present strain of black and tan hounds favoured by the Limerick Hunt from his own hounds and others introduced from the south-west of France in 1735. Christopher O'Sullivan, owner and editor of *The Limerick Echo*, described the oddly clad Royal Irish Constabulary as 'something one would associate with the Scarteen Hunt'. Mike Nono, the comedian, perpetuated this derogatory remark by referring to the new police auxiliaries as the Black and Tans from the stage of Limerick's Theatre Royal. (The Mulholland Collection)

The Limerick Hunt participating in a Limerick Show of the 1940s. The Normans probably introduced hunting from horseback with hounds into Ireland in much the same way as their ancestors had done in England. The hounds in the foreground are Scarteen foxhounds, better known as the famous Black and Tans. They were bred by the Ryan family of Ballyvistea, Emly, and later of Scarteen, Knocklong, who acquired their first foxhounds from a wrecked Armada ship off the Kerry coast in 1588. A receipt was issued by the Ryans in 1642, the earliest proof of their long trading record. (The Mulholland Collection)

This photograph dates from about 1900 and shows a group of men stacking timber on Harvey's Quay. The lock can be seen to their left, bounded by the wall of Wellesley Pier, a place better known today as Shannon Island, a man-made structure. The North Strand is located beyond the pier or island, stretching upriver to Thomond Bridge. It derived its name from its location, the more northerly of two strands on either side of Sarsfield Bridge. It was renamed in honour of George Clancy (1879–1921) who was murdered on 7 March 1921 while holding office as mayor. (The Waldron Collection)

This photograph of the Treaty Stone dates from about 1900, but the building in the background is of much more interest as it shows King John's Castle still serving as a garrison. A conical roof is visible on the tower to the left of the Treaty Stone, as well as part of the Georgian barracks dating from the early 1750s. Another barracks building can be seen to the right of the stone, but the tall building on the skyline may be located on the site occupied by the Castle Tavern. Note the fishing nets on the wall behind the stone. (The Waldron Collection)

This photograph of 1950 shows the Treaty Stone on an older location at the south-western corner of Thomond Bridge. The stone stood on the northern side of the bridge until 1865, when it was placed on a pedestal and installed here. It was moved to its present location on Clancy Strand, a short distance away, in 1990. According to folklore the Treaty of Limerick was signed on this rock which originally stood about halfway between the bridge and the Williamite camp. The first written records date to 1797 and 1808 and the stone was moved here in the early 1700s. (The Waldron Collection)

This waterfront scene, extending from Thomond Bridge to McGuire's Mills, dates from the early 1900s and was photographed from Honan's Quay. Martin Honan, a Limerick corn merchant, was elected as mayor in 1842 and 1843, as the Municipal Reform Act came into effect and deposed a corrupt corporation led by Charles Smith Vereker. Honan funded the building of a quay that extended from Wellesley Bridge to Arthurs' Quay and contributed generously to the soup kitchens during the Great Hunger of the 1840s. The rods beside the mooring-post would suggest that the barefooted boy was fishing. (The Waldron Collection)

This photograph, showing the waterfront from Thomond Bridge to Merchants' Quay, was taken from the vicinity of the swivel-bridge section of Sarsfield Bridge in the early 1900s. The building on the right stands at the corner of Harvey's Quay and Honan's Quay and bears a sign identifying it as a ship's chandler premises owned by a J. Howard. Ship chandlers dealt in canvas, cordage and other goods used by shipping craft. The single-storey building at the corner of the quay is not featured in William Corbett's *Map of the City of Limerick* (1865) but may be a Victorian toilet. (The Waldron Collection)

In this photograph of about 1900 one can see the western or riverside façade of King John's Castle and the size of the Georgian barracks buildings sheltering behind a medieval curtain wall. The North Strand was still, literally, a strand, and several boats are moored on both mud and shore as the tide was low when this photograph was taken. The Vikings introduced clinker-built wooden boats to the River Shannon soon after their arrival in the ninth century. The area from Thomond Bridge to the Curraghour Falls was a common fishery that the Abbey fishermen referred to as *Enuire*. (Tom Keogh Collection)

This view of Sarsfield Bridge dates from about 1950 and shows a number of boats moored off O'Callaghan Strand. The young boy seems to be entranced by the sailing vessel while, to his right, the seated man is engrossed in a book. The city was founded by the hardiest seafarers of all, the Vikings, and their settlement was once known as 'Limerick of the Swift Ships'. From 1524 onwards Limerick ships competed with those of Galway for the Spanish wine trade, and Henry VIII (1509–1547) had to intervene to restore peace between the two cities in 1536. (Limerick Museum)

This photograph dates from the early 1980s and shows King John's Castle with the twentieth-century corporation houses within its walls. The passageway in the right-hand corner is Curraghour Avenue which leads up to Doctor Hall's Alms-Houses or St Mary's Court, part of which is visible. The entire area to the left of the avenue now forms part of the City Hall car park and a new street, Castle Street, was constructed by the southern wall of King John's Castle. The Limerick Museum, sometimes called the Jim Kemmy Municipal Museum, is now located in the new street. (Barbara Bingham Collection)

This photograph dates from the early 1990s and shows a section of Clancy's Strand, formerly North Strand, extending from the Curraghour Falls to Thomond Gate. St Munchin's Catholic Church dates from 1922, replacing an earlier church erected in 1744. The Treaty Stone can be seen close to the bank of the river, a location to which it was moved in 1990. The Treaty Tavern can be seen in the upper right-hand corner, close to an arch of Thomond Bridge. The bridge was designed by James and George Pain and built between 1838 and 1840 to replace a medieval one. (Tom Keogh Collection)

This funeral, flanked by a Republican guard of honour, is proceeding across Thomond Bridge, having left St Munchin's Church on the corner of Clancy's Strand and High Road. The photograph was taken at the funeral of one of Commandant Edward 'Ned' Daly's sisters in the 1930s. Ned Daly (1891–1916) was the only boy and youngest child in a family of ten. He was born in Frederick Street, joined the Irish Volunteers and was executed following the Easter Rising. His sister, Kathleen (1879–1972), married Tom Clarke (1858–1916), the first signatory of the Proclamation of the Irish Republic. (Limerick Civic Trust)

This photograph shows the House of Industry on the North Strand, now Clancy's Strand, as it underwent restoration in the late 1990s. When legislation to establish workhouses and poorhouses came into effect in 1772, Joseph Johns, Mayor of Limerick, laid the foundation stone of this building on 10 March 1774. On 27 April 1786, Richard Crosbie (1755–c.1824) ascended by balloon from here and flew to Ballygirren, near Newmarket-on-Fergus, where he descended, the first recorded aerial flight from the banks of the Shannon. The building later became the Militia Barracks or Strand Barracks. (Tom Keogh Collection)

Kilrush Church derives its name from *Killrois*, *Cill Ruis* or *Cill Rois* (the church of the wood or promontory). This being the oldest ecclesiastical building within the city, it is also known as Old Church, St Munchin's Church or St Mainchin's Church. Located in a cul-de-sac off the North Circular Road, it may date from the tenth century. A brick buttress and frame supporting the western gable, with its flat-headed doorway, can be seen to the left. The Quinlivan family window, in the southern wall, may have come from an old friary in St Mary's Lane. (Tom Keogh Collection)

This postcard of the 1950s depicts the Ardhu House Hotel as it was about fifty years ago. The house was built by Thomas Revington, one of the first Limerick merchants to erect a department store building on the site now occupied by Roches Stores. He built Ardhu House soon after work commenced on Sarsfield Bridge in 1824. The Ennis Road was developed in the early 1830s. Ardhu House was later occupied by Robert de Ros Rose of Morgans, Askeaton and Ahabeg, Ballysimon Road. Ardhu House became a hotel, was renamed the Limerick Ryan and is now the Gresham Ardhu. (Tom Keogh Collection)

This steam vessel appears to be heading into the River Shannon from Russell's Quay which is now on the northern side of the new Shannon Bridge. John Norris Russell was a grain merchant, shipowner and industrialist whose commercial interests extended northwards into Ennis, where he had several grain stores. He built his Newtown Pery mills and his ships utilised the quay shown in the foreground of this postcard of about 1900. He had a linen warehouse in the former mansion of the Earl of Limerick, a store in Shannon Street and bought and demolished Mayoralty House in Quay Lane. (Tom Keogh Collection)

Two draymen pass along Steamboat Quay or Bishop's Quay in this photograph of about 1940. William Bulfin cycled throughout Ireland and covered about three thousand miles in a seven-month period in 1890. His articles appeared in *The United Irishman*, *Sinn Féin* and *The New York Daily News* before they were published as *Rambles in Ireland* (1907), with a preface by his friend, Aubrey de Vere. Bulfin noticed a poorly clad young man working as a docker in Limerick. He considered him an incarnation of the city's spirit, 'for Limerick, too, works hard . . . defiant of fate'. (Martin Breen Collection)

This photograph was taken during a Danus Trade Fair in either 1968 or 1969. The five people shown here are, from left to right, Tony O'Donovan, Bridget Daly, John Daly, Des Downes and Tony Grant. Tony O'Donovan was one of the directors of the Danus Clothing firm, along with his brothers, Donal and Noel, and sister, Maureen. John Daly and his wife, Bridget, had a clothing store in Ennis, and Des Downes was a commercial traveller. Tony Grant, a rugby player and Young Munster coach, then worked for Danus. He opened his own firm, Tower Carpets, in 1987. (Sean Daly)

This postcard of Kilkee dates from about 1900. One can see Victorian-style changing-huts on the strand and the West End is in the background. In 1833 Jonathan Binns of Lancashire was one of the assistant agricultural commissioners appointed to investigate poverty and compile a report. He eventually published *The Miseries and Beauties of Ireland* (1837). In Kilkee he recorded that the usual curraghs, or canoes, favoured by the fishermen were covered 'with tarred canvas instead of hides', possibly for the sake of economy, and were manufactured at prices ranging from twenty to thirty shillings (€1.27 to €1.90). (The Waldron Collection)

This photograph of Kilkee dates from the first decade of the twentieth century. In 1890 a French travel writer, Marie Anne de Bovet, visited Kilkee. Her book, *Trois Mois en Irlande*, was translated as *Three Months in Kilkee* (1891) by Mrs Arthur Walter. 'Like every other place,' the later Marie Anne Marchioness Deschamp de Bois Herbert wrote, 'it is given up to pleasant indolence . . . There are a few machines drawn up on the beach for the use of bathers. Men are forbidden to bathe after an hour so early that most prefer to go out some way along the coast.' (The Waldron Collection)

This view of Kilkee's West End can be dated to 1950. Sean O'Faolain wrote of his own experiences as a commercial traveller who visited Kilkee about three times every winter. He recalled how the porters at Ennistymon would add ballast to the small, almost empty carriages of the West Clare Railway to prevent them being blown off the tracks. When the summer season was over and the Limerick visitors returned home, Kilkee became a ghost town throughout the winter months. Winter may have been approaching when this photograph was taken, as most of the people shown appear to be well wrapped up. (Martin Breen Collection)

In this photograph of about 1900 a man views the secne from Knockroe Point which overlooks Intrinsic Bay and Illaunawhilla, possibly an anglicisation of *Oileán an Fuile* (the island of sin, trace or sign). Knockroe Point takes its name from *Cnoc Ruadh* (the red or brown hill). Intrinsic Bay derives its name from a ship that was wrecked on Bishop's Island, three and a quarter miles south-west of Knockroe Point, on 30 January 1836. The *Intrinsic* was carrying a cargo of iron and steel from Liverpool to New Orleans when she was lost along with her crew of fifteen. (The Waldron Collection)

Cliff scenery is one of Kilkee's greatest natural attractions. In this photograph of the early 1900s a man can be seen to the left and a group of two men and two women to the right of the Amphitheatre. In 1836 Mary John Knott described this feature close to the reef known as the Duggerna Rock: 'Very near the juncture of this reef with the south point of the bay is a large rude opening, nearly circular, with projecting shelves of rock, resembling benches and floors around at different heights, and contracting as they descend like an amphitheatre.' (The Waldron Collection)

The promenade in Kilkee extends from the strand area on the left, around by the West End and finishes near the Pollock Holes. This photograph was taken from the eastern end of the bay about 1900. William Whittaker Barry, lawyer by profession and pedestrian by choice, visited Kilkee in September 1864. 'About a mile from the town I met three well-dressed young ladies,' he wrote, 'as sure harbingers of a watering-place as swallows of spring . . . The town consists of two or three back streets but principally of fine rows of houses, extending round nearly the whole bay.' (The Waldron Collection)

The placid appearance of the strand is due to a line of rocks that stretch across one-third of Moore Bay and protect the sheltered bathing area shown in this photograph of the early 1900s. The waters outside the reef formed by the Duggerna Rocks are dangerous for shipping; at least eight ships were wrecked between 1814 and 1888. These wrecks included the brig, *Aurora*, in October 1814. It actually sank off Loop Head but some survivors landed in Kilkee. The emigrant barque, *Edmund*, ran on to the Duggerna Rocks and ninety-six passengers drowned on 20 November 1850. (The Waldron Collection)

The Newfoundout was, and is, a swimming area to the east of the Duggerna Rocks that was discovered or 'newly found out' by the Limerick swimmers patronising Victorian Kilkee. This postcard dating from the 1940s shows a diver who has just launched himself from the diving board in front of an admiring audience. Major Reginald Evelyn Peter Southhouse Cheyney (1896–1951) was the son of Dr George Cheyney of Waver, Hertfordshire, and Gertrude E. Studdert, the daughter of Jonas Studdert, Atlantic House, Kilkee. He is best known under his pen-name, Peter Cheyney, and was born in Atlantic House. He was a member of the O'Donnell family, who owned much of Kilkee, including the Newfoundout. (The Waldron Collection)

This photograph dates from September 1916 and shows two children paddling in the water at Kilkee. The young girl is Mary 'Kit' Waldron and the boy is her brother, Aidan, aged eight. Kit Waldron married Seamus Daltun, the chief translator in Leinster House, the man responsible for translating all the statutes into Irish. Aidan Waldron became a member of the Royal College of Veterinary Surgeons. Peter Cheyney's birthplace, Atlantic House, was on the northern shore of the bay which is visible in the background. It was used as a coastguard station in the early 1900s before it was demolished. (The Waldron Collection)

The Limerick Soviet was partly organised by Robert 'Bobby' Byrne who was killed on 6 April 1919. He did not live long enough to see his plan come into effect, from Monday, 14 April, until Saturday, 26 April 1919. A series of postcards was published to commemorate his death. These showed various scenes from his funeral procession, but the success of the soviet owed more to the presence of a large gathering of international journalists in the city. They had come to Limerick to report on the preparations for a transatlantic flight which a Major Woods had proposed to undertake. (The Waldron Collection)

This photograph dates from about 1920 and shows John and Mary Waldron outside 4 Verona Esplanade, off O'Connell Avenue, Limerick. Verona locates William Shakespeare's play, *The Two Gentlemen of Verona*, and the name of Verona Esplanade may have been inspired by this play. Pope Pius IX was supported by the people of Limerick during his wars with the King of Italy and the French Emperor. The city contributed more money and men to the Pope than any other place in Ireland during 1860. Limerick members of the Irish Papal Brigade fought at Ancona, Spoleto, Perugia and Castel Fidardo, and they may have brought the name of Verona Esplanade home with them. (The Waldron Collection)

There are two Waldron families shown in this photograph of 1917. Paddy and John Waldron were identical twins and their wives were, respectively, Lil and Ciss. Ciss is the first lady on the left in the back row with her son, Paddy Waldron, in her arms. Lil is next to her, holding Thomas Waldron, and standing beside Aidan Waldron, Ciss's older son. This family surname appears in Irish as *de Bhaldraithe*, the form adopted by Máire, the first girl on the left in the front row. She married Máirtín Ó Flathartaigh who was secretary of the President's office for over thirty years. (The Waldron Collection)

This photograph of the young Pádraig de Bhaldraithe, taken with his mother, Ciss, can be dated to about 1920. Pádraig's first cousin, Thomas, was professor of Modern Irish Language and Literature in University College Dublin, and author of *The Irish of Cois Fhairrge: A Phonetic Study* (1945) and *Gaeilge Chois Fhairrge: An Deilbhíocht* (1953), and consultant editor of the *English-Irish Dictionary* (1978). Pádraig de Bhaldraithe qualified as a batchelor of law and has amassed a large collection of family memorabilia, papers, photographs, postcards and programmes, which is of particular interest to historians. (The Waldron Collection)

In this photograph of the 1930s one can see Ciss Waldron and her aunt, Elizabeth Keogh, née Clancy, of Killard, taking the sea air and sea spray as they stroll along the promenade at Kilkee. Elizabeth Keogh and her brother, George Clancy, owned a drapery store at 48 William Street, Limerick. The shop was destroyed by fire in 1913 in which their nephew, from Kilkee, lost his life. The premises was rebuilt and was later taken over by Harry Keogh, Elizabeth's son and George Clancy's nephew. (The Waldron Collection)

This photograph shows Mary 'Kit' Waldron standing at the railings of 4 Verona Esplanade, about 1920. Her surname has appeared in Irish variously as *Ualðrán*, *MacUalðráin*, *MacBhalðráin*, *MacUalronta*, *MacBhalronta*, *MacUailðrín*, *MacUailtrín*, *MacBhailðrín* and *MacBhailtrín*. *MacBhalronta* (meaning the son of Waleran), an Anglo-Saxon personal name, and a hibernicised patronymic surname adopted by the family of Wesley in Leinster. Waldron is also a variant form of the Old English local name Waldern or Walderne, meaning the house in a forest, open woodland or waste ground, a place in Sussex, England. (The Waldron Collection)

This group photograph which dates from about 1900 was taken on the steps of the monument in the People's Park. Three of the four women can be identified. From left to right, the first lady is Elizabeth Keogh, née Clancy, next to her is Lil MacNamara who married Paddy Waldron, and on the extreme right is Ciss MacNamara who married John Waldron. The young girl in front is May Keogh, Elizabeth's daughter. The Earl of Limerick presented the Corporation with a conditional 500-year lease of the park which opened in August 1877. (The Waldron Collection)

This photograph dates from about 1900 and shows Ciss Waldron with the children of Elizabeth Keogh, née Clancy, outside their Limerick home. The boy's name is Harry and the girl is May. The Keogh surname is a derivative of *Mac Eochadha* and its variant forms, *Mac Ceoch*, *Mac Ceothach* and *Mac Eothach* (the son of *Eochaidh*), a common personal name in ancient Ireland. There were four distinct families of *Mac Eoghadha*: one originated in Owney, County Tipperary; the second originated in Moylurg, County Roscommon; and the others were branches of the O'Byrnes of Leinster and the O'Kelly's of Ui Maine. (The Waldron Collection)

This photograph shows Brother Looney with an inter-league team from Sexton Street during the 1960s. Tom Keogh Snr was the photographer who captured this scene at the Christian Brothers' playing field at Rathbane. The first, second and fifth hurlers from the left in the back row are, respectively, Benny Fitzgerald, Eddie Tobin and Mike Kenny. The first, fifth and sixth hurlers in the middle row are, from the left, respectively, Cha Hearn, Tommy Hanrahan and Pat Cooney. All the boys were members of the seventh class in the Christian Brothers' Primary School. (Tom Keogh Collection)

This photograph was taken by Tom Keogh from the doorway of the Jim Kemmy Municipal Museum which is better known as the Limerick Museum. The man in the foreground is Willy Ryan, a local man who was badly injured in a lawn mower accident several years previously. The crook or stick in his right hand is a walking aid. He uses the spotless wheelbarrow as a shopping-trolley for heavy messages and is rarely seen without his dog. The building in the background is the south-eastern corner of King John's Castle and the car is Tom Keogh's. (Tom Keogh Collection)

The man wearing the mayoral chain of office is John Daly (1846–1916). He is photographed here with a group of local representatives known collectively as the Limerick Labour Corporation of 1899. John Daly was a Fenian and an Irish Republican Brotherhood leader when he was arrested in Birkenhead, England, on 11 April 1884. He was sentenced to life imprisonment for carrying explosives but was released after serving over twelve years in jail. He was the first modern political prisoner to revive the use of the hunger strike as a weapon against the English. He was Mayor in 1899, 1900 and 1901. (Limerick Museum)

In this photograph of the 1940s three young girls are sitting beneath a statue of Christ in the grounds of Laurel Hill Convent. Peggy Millar is on the left and Jean Mulholland in the centre. Mother D'Hover, superioress of the Faithful Companions of Jesus, founded the convent in 1854. She was helped by Brother J. P. Welsh of the Christian Brothers who helped her acquire the site. Kate O'Brien (1897–1974) is probably the convent's most famous pupil. She was a local girl from Mulgrave Street, best remembered as a novelist, playwright, journalist and critic. (The Mulholland Collection)

World War II was known as 'the Emergency' in Ireland, but life continued almost as usual for the majority of Irish people. Lack of fuel, especially petrol and diesel, however, meant that there were restrictions on how far people could travel. All sorts of transport came into use, especially during the holiday season. Drivers would hoard petrol for a long journey and use alternative transport on arrival. Bernard and Mary Frances Mulholland of William Street, Limerick, are shown here with their daughters, Myriam, Jean, Biddy and Margaret, and some local children, using a horse and cart during a Kerry holiday. (The Mulholland Collection)

The Catholic Church achieved power, control and social position by supporting the British Government in nineteenth-century Ireland. This was reflected in Limerick city, particularly during the episcopate (1886–1917) of Edward Thomas O'Dwyer which spanned the late nineteenth and the early twentieth century. Power was retained by the Church's support of the emerging Irish Free State but perverted as the bishops turned the new state into a theocracy. Confraternities and other religious societies were mobilised and manipulated by cynical churchmen. These Legion of Mary members of the 1950s, however, were unaware of any agenda — people were innocent then. (The Mulholland Collection)

Kilkee, although part of County Clare, is regarded as a suburb of Limerick city, a status acknowledged by Kilkee itself. In the 1950s this happy group was photographed outside the Hydro Hotel. Biddy and Jean Mulholland, Maeve and Joan Green, all from Limerick, and the McCanns of Dundalk are featured here. August was the traditional holiday month for the more affluent members of Limerick society to gather in the West Clare resort, a tradition established almost two centuries earlier. July was the next most popular month, followed by June and September. The more prosperous families stayed for three months. (The Mulholland Collection)

The Laurel Hill Preparatory School pupils who posed for this photograph in the 1940s are: (*front row, left to right*) Kathleen Costelloe, Kathleen Butler, Jean Mulholland, Venna Larkin and Elinor MacNamara; (*second row*) Kitty Heffernan, Gertrude Quinn, Ita Moloney, Maureen Meaney and Kathleen Meaney; (*third row*) Celine Wallace, Eithne Slattery, Peggy Millar, Sheila Raleigh, one unidentified girl, Vera Holland and Peggy Raleigh; (*back row*) unidentified girl, Mary Fitzgerald, (?) Thompson, Clare Millar and Kate Carroll. The convent grounds are visible in the background. (The Mulholland Collection)

John and Ciss Waldron are seen here walking along the Strand Line in Kilkee in the 1940s. In 1832, a century earlier, Mary John Knott mentioned how the village of a few years previously was the residence of fishermen whose homes formed a row of cottages known as Old Kilkee. She went on to describe the 'new town' assuming a semicircular form, following the curve of the beach or strand, the Strand Line. She mentioned that the West End contained the most modern houses and accommodation and recorded that there were even some such houses in the 'village'. (The Waldron Collection)

The Limerick Steamship Company at their stand at the Limerick Horse Show in the 1950s. Originally known as the London and Limerick Steamship Company when it was established in the 1850s, it became a separate entity, the Limerick Steamship Company, in 1893. In 1969 it amalgamated with Palgrave Murphy to form Hibernian Transport, which went into liquidation towards the end of 1970. The four ladies posing at the exhibition counter are, from left to right, Jean Mulholland, Mary Fitzgerald, Eileen Fitzgerald and Biddy Mulholland. The Limerick Show is still held at the same venue, the Greenpark Racecourse. (The Mulholland Collection)

This photograph dates from about 1900 and shows the Keogh family posing outside their Limerick home. An interesting facet on the social history of the time might lead one to query the Keogh family's relationship with their servants. A girl in a maid's outfit and a man wearing a cap appear to be posing in the background from behind the lowered window. The man in front is James P. Keogh, the husband of Elizabeth Clancy, with their children Harry and May. Elizabeth does not appear here as it is Ciss Waldron who is standing to the right. (The Waldron Collection)

This studio portrait of Elizabeth Keogh and her children, Harry and May, dates from about 1900. The most unusual feature of this particular photograph is the fact that the young boy is wearing a dress. In ancient times people believed that the fairies would spirit away male children and leave a changeling to replace the lost boy. By dressing a boy in girls' clothing people could confuse the fairies, a tradition which continued into the 1930s throughout the west of Ireland. Hygiene was a consideration as well. (The Waldron Collection)

Four generations of the O'Mara family are represented in this photograph of about 1900. The O'Maras were one of four families that dominated the bacon trade in Limerick city, the others being the Dennys, Mattersons and Shaws. This last family had a premises close to Limerick Prison and the expression referring to someone as being 'at the back of Shaws' meant that the person was in prison. James O'Mara (1873–1948) was a member of the Irish Parliamentary Party until 1907. He supported Sinn Féin and the Irish Volunteers and was elected to the first Dáil Éireann. (The Waldron Collection)

This photograph of the Limerick Post Office hockey team dates back to 1905: (*back row, left to right*) T. Gale, Paddy Waldron, J. Reynolds, J. Tierney, R. Byrne and John Waldron; (*middle row*) F. Humphries, D. Kelly, F. Clifford, P. Curran and M. O'Callaghan; (*front*) M. Sheedy and R. M. MacNamara. Hockey is considered to be of English origin and was not promoted by the Gaelic Athletic Association even though it may have evolved from hurling or shinty. (The Waldron Collection)

This photograph was taken on Whit Monday 1905. It features a group of people taking an excursion from Limerick to Killaloe by long car, a long horse-drawn cart that could accommodate at least the thirteen people shown here, including Frank Clifford and his sister, Molly, from William Street. Frank is the man in the foreground, second seat from the right, looking towards the camera. Killaloe was a popular resort for city people as it was only twelve miles from Limerick. Visitors could return home the same day, although the journey could take about three hours each way. (The Waldron Collection)

The Jesuit cricket team of 1907 is featured in this photograph. The cricket club was formed by Fr Lockington, J. Walshe, J. O'Keefe, J. O'Sullivan, W. Halpin, T. Treacy, T. Buckley and Thomas Waldron. Membership was confined to members of the Ignatius Sodality, a confraternity group, and the members used the grounds of Crescent College for practice. Fr Lockington later published a book, *The Soul of Ireland* (1919), an examination of the spiritual life of the country at that period. Cricket was played at the Catholic Institute grounds in Rossbrien, a venue that was used by other clubs and associations. (The Waldron Collection)

This photograph shows the National League Championship winners of 1934. The team members were Tim Ryan (capt.), Dave Clohessy, Paddy Clohessy, Jim Close, Mick Cross, Ned Cregan, Garret Howard, Michael Kennedy, John Mackey, Mick Mackey, Tom McCarthy, Mick Ryan, Jim Roche, P. Scanlan and Jackie O'Donnell. Limerick won this championship for four years in a row, 1933–36. The first winning team was captained by Micky Fitzgibbon, the second and third teams by Tim Ryan, and Mick Mackey captained the fourth. Limerick won fifty-eight games out of sixty-five between 1933 and 1938. (The Waldron Collection)

This photograph was taken by Roy McCormack, most likely in the late 1960s when this terrace of Georgian housing at Ellen Street was extensively renovated. The Ideal Shoe Service at No. 12 became Robin O'Donnell's Ellen Street Antiques until he retired in 2003. The next building, No. 13, houses another antiques store, Portabello Antiques, which was opened by Pauline Fenton in 1984. Michael Richardson ran Limerick's first pirate radio station, Big L, from No. 13, formerly the Clancy home. Jim Kemmy, Kevin Hannan, Eamon O'Connor and Tony Browne were among the people interviewed here by Michael Richardson. (Barbara Bingham Collection)

The Limerick Dairies are shown in this photograph of about 1950, the year in which the Irish Creamery Milk Suppliers' Association was founded. Thomas Henry Cleeve (1844–1908), a Canadian, arrived in Limerick in 1864. He became interested in Irish agriculture and persuaded his brothers to join him. They established creameries and opened factories to process the cream and skimmed milk. They employed almost one thousand people in the city as they had several creameries, a condensed milk factory, a toffee factory, a box factory and a cooperage. The first co-operative creamery was founded in Dromcolliher in 1890. (The Mulholland Collection)

Excursions from Limerick to Killaloe and places of interest were usually undertaken by long car, an elongated trap or horse-drawn vehicle. With the advent of a railway line connecting Limerick with Dublin from May 1848 onwards, the coaching trade could have collapsed almost completely. Charles Bianconi (1785–1875) had made a fortune from the coaching business, but he adapted to the changing circumstances. He became a railway director in 1834 and used his coaches to service the stops between the new railway stations. His rivals followed his example to survive and remain in business, as did this long car of 1900. (The Waldron Collection)

During their school holidays in the 1940s these school friends liked to explore the River Shannon. They are, from left to right, Marie Crowe, Jean Mulholland, Elinor MacNamara and Venna Larkin. The photograph appears to have been taken at Worrall's End, a small quay on the river half a mile from the modern pump house at Castleconnell. The quay and surrounding area derived its name from a family who once lived here, the Worralls. Worrall is an Old English local name meaning the nook or valley of bog-myrtle. Worrall's End is sometimes misnamed as World's End or Worrall's Inn. (The Mulholland Collection)

A postcard of the 1940s describes this part of Laurel Hill Convent as a day school and technical kitchen. It is close to the main entrance and is accessible from the avenue to which it gives its name, Laurel Hill Avenue. Kate O'Brien (1897–1974) was a pupil here until 1916. She was influenced by the Reverend Mother, a Londoner of the hidebound upper-class English type who had little time for the Gaelic Revival. She was, however, a match for Bishop Edward Thomas O'Dwyer, as he had no authority over herself or her convent, a French foundation. (The Mulholland Collection)

Sarah O'Malley wrote the obituary for Standish 'Stan' Stewart in the *North Munster Antiquarian Journal* of 1966 and 1967. She described him as a chemist by profession, a photographer of note and a scholar and antiquarian by choice. This photograph of the 1960s shows Marie Keogh, Stan Stewart's assistant, using a glazer to put a shine on the old black and white photographs in Stan's workshop, part of his chemist's in O'Connell Street. Stan Stewart was a personal friend of Michael O'Donovan (1903–1966), the writer better known as Frank O'Connor. (Tom Keogh Collection)

In the 1940s Scoil A of Laurel Hill Convent presented a school play in which this group of schoolgirls played various roles. The five girls in the background are, from left to right, Elinor MacNamara, Carmel Downes, Kathleen Butler, Marie Crowe and Eileen Keane. The two fan-wielding ladies in the foreground are Nuala McPolin and Myriam Mulholland. The dancing costumes worn by four of the girls were popularised during the Gaelic Revival. In Kate O'Brien's days four nuns, Mother Lelia Ferguson, Mother Sabina Ferguson, (Lelia's younger sister), Mother Maria ffrench and Mother Thecla Patterson, were considered rebels. (The Mulholland Collection)

Stan Stewart cycled all over County Limerick with Michael and Evelyn O'Donovan in May 1940. At one point a friendly hotel owner informed Stan that the police were investigating the couple, thinking that they were German spies. The pair returned for another cycling tour of the west of Ireland in June, became exhausted after about two weeks and returned to Limerick where they stayed in Stan's house on Shelbourne Road. In the 1960s Marie Keogh posed for this photograph in Stan's show rooms which were over the shop. Reverse the image on the window to read Stewart's Show Rooms. (Tom Keogh Collection)

Stan Stewart photographed 67 Mungret Street about 1950. The name M. Hayes appears on the fascia board above the window and business was conducted here by Patrick Hayes in 1913. Edmund Hayes owned an adjoining premises at No. 66 in 1913. Mungret Street derived its name from a defended gateway, Mungret Gate, which was one of the guarded entrances to the walled city. A large market area evolved around the vicinity of the gate, which was demolished about 1823, probably by Major Hodges Maunsell. The foundation stone of the gate was placed in the riverside façade of the Plassey Mill. (Martin Breen Collection)

Roches Stores opened in Limerick in 1937 in the former McBirney premises at the corner of Sarsfield Street and O'Connell Street. The business purchased by Roches Stores occupied 134 and 135 O'Connell Street and 28, 29 and 30 Sarsfield Street. A fire started in the basement and destroyed the entire building in 1947. The firm continued to trade from the former staff quarters, the Badminton Hall, while some of their workers were employed in Cork and Dublin branches. Roy McCormack photographed the rebuilding of Roches Stores which re-opened for business again in 1951. (Barbara Bingham Collection)

This photograph, taken by Roy McCormack, shows New Road in Thomondgate as it looked in the mid-1970s. The name New Road pre-dates the later Sexton Street North which was named after Edmund Sexton Pery (1719–1806). He owned land to the north of New Road. Martin O'Halloran's bar is visible on the right, one of the first pubs in Thomondgate to become a lounge bar. One part of the pub floor was tiled, while the other was carpeted. Anyone ordering from the carpet had to pay lounge bar prices! (Barbara Bingham Collection)

Crowe's Bar was located on the corner of Lord Edward Street and Carey's Road, opposite the People's Park. This photograph dates from the 1940s and shows a row of houses that has since disappeared. Lord Edward Street is more familiarly called Edward Street today and commemorates Lord Edward Fizgerald (1763–1798). He was killed by Major Henry Charles Sirr as he resisted arrest during the 1798 Rebellion. Lord Edward's daughter, Pamela, married Sir Guy Campbell (1786–1848) of Plassy and was buried in the graveyard of Kilmurry Church in 1869. Carey's Road commemorates Joseph Carey, a charitable Victorian doctor. (Tom Keogh Collection)

Roy McCormack photographed the remains of this terrace on New Road, Thomondgate, in the mid-1970s. Since then parts of Thomondgate have changed almost beyond recognition. The Northern Ring Road now connects the Cratloe Road junction with Ivan's Cross, a distinct improvement on driving across a few muddy fields at Caherdavin, where motorists pioneered a new trail in the 1970s. At the end of the ruined terrace, beyond the electricity pole, is Bill Burke's public house, the Ardnacrusha Bar. The bar is located at 22 New Road, owned by the same family and trading under the same name. (Barbara Bingham Collection)

This photograph can be dated to between 1930 and 1935. It shows the staff of a butter factory, that of W. C. McDonnell, standing outside the premises at, most likely, Roches' Street. The firm was established by William and Charles McDonnell, is listed in several trade directories issued between 1875 and 1938, and owned two other premises at Sexton Street and Thomas Street. Roches' Street derives its name from Thomas and William Roche, two dealers in provisions in Dominic Street, who opened a bank in 1801. They sold their Limerick Bank to the new Provincial Bank in 1825. (Tom Keogh Collection)

Limerick people have been travelling to Kilkee for their annual holidays since the early 1800s. Initially they travelled by steamboat to Kilrush where they disembarked at Cappa Pier. They travelled on to Kilkee by pony and trap or jaunting car and frequently hired another cart or vehicle to ferry their luggage. The opening of the West Clare Railway changed the mode of travel, but not the destination, from 1892 to 1961. This photograph shows part of the West End, to the right, as it looked in 1900. Note the pony and trap in the foreground with a pony and cart behind. (The Waldron Collection)

In 1691 a Jacobite army of 25,000 under the command of General Charles Chalmont, Marquis de Saint-Ruth, opposed 18,000 Williamite troops led by General Godert de Ginkel (1630–1703), against the advice of Patrick Sarsfield who had held Limerick, successfully, during the siege of 1690. In the ensuing Battle of Aughrim the Jacobites were defeated and retreated to Limerick. In 1991 Cormac Hurley, along with the non-denominational Scout Association of Ireland (1908) and the Catholic Boy Scouts of Ireland (1927), two Limerick scout troops and other volunteers, re-enacted Sarsfield's retreat to Limerick to raise funds for St Gabriel's School. (Gerry O'Donovan)

This view of Mathew Bridge, the Abbey river, Bank Place and Charlotte's Quay was photographed by Roy McCormack in the late 1980s. The Granary, to the right of the car park shown on the extreme left, was built soon after Philip Roche purchased the site in 1787. It was used as a bonding warehouse into the 1970s. The Limerick City Library, Limerick's treasure house of local history, is located in the Granary. It is one of the two most user-friendly libraries in Ireland. (Barbara Bingham Collection)

This view of Merchants' Quay with St Augustine Place in the background dates from the 1960s. The County Courthouse on the left dates from 1810 and was extensively renovated in 2002. The letters EARY'S to the right of the courthouse indicate where Geary's biscuit factory was located. The Women's Gaol, facing towards the camera, was then in use as a tax office and has been replaced by the new City Hall since 1990. The Treaty Stone, however, never stood in this location. Its insertion here is part of a collage designed when Limerick Corporation was planning to move it. (Tom Keogh Collection)